The Write TEEN Words

Poetry, quotes and titles
for all of life's adolescent moments

Selected by
Crystal Dawn Perry

ClearSky Publishing
Hixson, Tennessee

A special thanks to the contributing poets for giving of themselves and their work to this compilation. Every effort has been made to give proper credit for each poem and quote. In the event of any question, we regret the error and will be glad to give proper credit in future editions of this book. The Bible scriptures are from the New King James Version and the New International Version.

> The Write Teen Words
> ClearSky Publishing
> P.O. Box 606-B
> Hixson, TN 37343

Copyright ©2007 ClearSky Publishing

All Rights Reserved. No part of this product may be reproduced or distributed in any form including commercial purposes or by electronic means. Law strictly forbids distribution without prior written permission of the publisher.

With purchase, permission is granted to reproduce verses from this book, on a limited basis, for personal use only.

> Printed in the United States of America.

> The Write TEEN Words

> ISBN 978-0-9706381-7-5

I dedicate this book to Cody and Chandler Brooks. I love you.

Breathe-in experience,
breathe-out poetry.
-Muriel Rukeyser

**A few suggestions for
getting the most out of**

The Write TEEN Words

- ❖ The verses in this book are meant to provide ideas as well as inspire them. Use the blank lines provided after each topic in the title section and after the poetry and quote sections to write your own words or favorite verses. Forget what you've learned about not writing in books. This is your book and you should write down your ideas so you'll have a good idea when you need it. More good ideas are forgotten than are remembered.

- ❖ Cross-references are used when the verses for another topic apply but are too numerous to repeat under both headings. The cross-references will direct you to another topic within the same section. For example, if you are considering a title about "Friends" you will be cross-referenced to "Multiples," also in the title section. Consider verses from both topics even if you don't think they will apply. They usually will.

- ❖ Use your imagination. Don't be afraid to change or omit a few words to suit your needs. These verses are for your personal use – personalize them!

Tips to personalize your pages:

Scrapbooks are a great way to share memories and tell stories. An interesting title will capture the reader's attention and a meaningful poem or quote is the perfect way to convey emotions. Below are some ideas to help you personalize your pages using your own words or the verses found in this book.

- Title a page with your subject's nickname. Include journaling to tell the story behind the nickname and who began it.
- If you are not confident in your handwriting, scatter the words across the page being careful to keep the phrase readable. This will draw your eyes across the layout and it won't matter if the words are perfectly straight.
- Create a page about your home life and include your full address.
- Use two or more words that start with the same letter or sound. Try this with your subject's name and a character trait.

    Example: Cody's Clique or Jumpy Jack
- Use a quote overheard at the day's event. Was something said that made everybody laugh? Write it down before you forget it.
- Cut words from a school program or newspaper or include the entire program to include dates, names, type of event, etc.
- Write the name of a popular song for your title or journal using meaningful lyrics. Don't forget to include your "special song" if you have one.
- Include a page from your personal journal or blog.
- Use the title of a favorite book. For an authentic appearance, use vellum to trace the letters from the book cover.

- Use each letter of the person's name to start a phrase describing his or her personality.

  Example:

  Champion volleyball player

  Hates pink

  Always on the phone

  Never wears the same thing twice

  Daring

  Late to bed, late to school

  Easy to start laughing

  Rules the pitcher mound

- Title your page with a common phrase used by the subject. If the person uses it consistently throughout the day, express this by repeating it several times across the page.

  Example: "Whatever!"

- Include Slang. This will be interesting in future years.

- Make a Top Ten list. This will make for easier journaling because it will not need to be in complete sentences or paragraph form.

  Example: Top Ten Things that Make Me Laugh

- Look beyond the people and tangible items in your photographs. What does this picture make you think about? Maybe you are seeing an "Attitude" or "Beauty." Use these descriptions as keys when searching topics.

- Write around the edge of a photograph or around the edge of the page. If the writing extends beyond where it began, keep writing above or below the text, creating a swirl effect; it will not matter where it ends. If the end of the writing does not meet the beginning, fill in the empty space with embellishment. Repeat the embellishment elsewhere on the page so it is not an obvious "space-filler."

- Record an especially meaningful poem, quote or lyric even if it doesn't correspond to a particular photograph. Copy the verse onto the page and then start writing about the emotions and memories it brings to mind. With or without a picture scrapbooks can capture memories and tell a story.

Table Of Contents
for all of life's adolescent moments

	Titles	Poems	Quotes
Adoption/Foster Child	2	78	164
Adoption/Foster Child	2	78	164
Amusement Park	2	78	164
Anguish/Despondency	2	78	165
Animal/Pet	3	80	166
Arts/Crafts	3	80	167
Attitude/Ego	4	81	167
Aunt	4	81	168
Babysitting	4	81	168
Band/Musical Instruments	5	82	169
Baseball	5	83	170
Basketball	6	83	171
Beach	6	84	171
Beauty	7	84	172
Bedroom	7	84	172
Birthday	8	85	173
Books	9	86	174
Bowling	9	86	174
Boxing/Fighting	9	86	174
Boyfriend	10	87	175
Boys	10	87	175
Braces	11	88	176
Break-up	11	88	177
Brother	12	89	178
Camping	12	90	179
Car/Driving	13	90	179
Cat	14	92	181
Character/Personality Traits	15	93	181

	Titles	Poems	Quotes
Cheerleading	16	94	183
Child	16	94	183
Chores	16	94	183
Christmas	17	95	184
Clothes	17	95	185
Clubs/Committee/Leadership	17	95	185
College	18	96	186
Computer	18	96	187
Cousin	19	97	187
Dance	19	97	188
Dating	20	98	188
Daughter	21	99	190
Diet	21	100	191
Discipline/Grounding	22	100	191
Dog	22	101	192
Do-it-yourself/Handiwork	22	101	192
Drama/School Program	23	101	193
Dreams/Goals/Ambition	23	102	194
Easter	24	103	195
Exchange Student	24	103	196
Excitement/Extreme Sports/Fear	25	104	196
Exercise/Physique	25	104	197
Face	25	104	198
Family/Heritage	26	105	198
Father	27	106	200
Fishing	27	—	201
Football	28	107	202
Friends/Best Friend	28	107	202
Friends-long distance	29	108	205
Fun/Silliness	29	109	205
Games	30	109	207
Gift	30	109	207

	Titles	Poems	Quotes
Girls	30	110	208
Girlfriend	31	111	209
Glasses/Contacts	31	111	209
Golf	32	111	209
Graduation	32	112	210
Grandchild/Grandparent	33	113	211
Growing Up	33	114	212
Gymnastics	34	115	214
Habit	34	115	214
Hair	35	115	214
Half–sibling	35	116	215
Halloween	35	116	216
Handicap	36	117	216
Hang-out/Special Place	36	117	216
Hanukkah	36	—	216
Happiness	37	117	217
Hardship	37	118	218
Hobby/Collection	37	118	219
Hockey	38	118	219
Home	38	119	220
Home School	39	119	221
Homecoming	40	119	221
Hope Chest	40	—	221
Hug/Kiss	40	120	221
Hunting	41	120	222
Illness/Injury	41	120	223
Independence	42	122	223
Independence Day	42	122	225
Job	43	123	225
Laziness	43	123	225
Life/EveryDay Moments	44	123	226
Love	44	124	228

	Titles	Poems	Quotes
Make-up	45	127	230
Martial Arts	46	—	230
Memories	46	127	231
Memory of a Loved One	46	127	232
Military	47	128	233
Money	48	129	233
Mother	48	129	234
Motorcycle	49	—	236
Movies/Television	49	130	236
Multiples	50	130	237
Music	50	131	237
Nature	51	—	238
New Year	51	131	239
Off-Road	52	—	239
Parade	52	132	240
Parent	52	133	240
Parent/Child Relationship	53	133	242
Party	53	135	243
Passover	54	136	244
Prom	54	136	244
Rock-Climbing	54	136	244
Running	55	137	245
School	55	137	245
Scouts	56	—	247
Scrapbooking	56	138	247
Shopping	57	138	248
Sibling	57	139	248
Sister	58	140	249
Skateboarding	58	141	251
Skating	59	141	251
Skiing	59	141	251
Sleepover	59	142	252

	Titles	Poems	Quotes
Snow	60	142	252
Soccer	60	142	252
Softball	61	143	253
Son	61	143	253
Special Needs	62	144	254
Sports/Games	62	144	255
Spring Break	63	145	257
St. Patrick's Day	64	146	257
Step-Parent/Step-Sibling	64	146	257
Style	64	147	258
Summer	65	148	259
Sunbathing	66	148	260
Sunglasses	66	148	260
Surfing	66	149	260
Swimming/Water Sports	67	149	260
Talent	67	150	261
Tattoo/Piercing	68	—	263
Teenager	68	150	263
Telephone	69	152	266
Tennis/Racquetball	70	153	266
Thanksgiving	70	153	267
Tradition	70	154	267
Travel	71	154	268
Trouble	71	154	268
Uncle	72	155	269
Vacation	72	155	269
Valentine's Day	72	156	270
Volleyball	73	157	270
Volunteer Work	73	157	270
Work	73	157	271
Wrestling	74	158	272
Yard Work	74	158	272

Titles are but nicknames,
and every nickname is a title.
-Thomas Paine

Titles

Adoption/Foster Child
From One Heart to Another
TRUST
My Promise to You
From Broken Home to Mended Heart
My Adoption Story
A New Beginning
A Dream Come True
A Fresh Start
A Place to Call Home
Together Forever

Amusement Park
One Track Mind
AmuseMEnt
What Goes Up Must Come Down
Fear Factor
Maximum Velocity

Anguish/Despondency
Love Hurts
Broken Dreams, Broken Heart
HOPE
Personal Demons
Contents Under Pressure
A Force of Nature
Where There is Love, There is Hope
PAIN
Touched by an Anger

Animal/Pet
(see also Cat and Dog)

A Pet Project
Flea Market
Party Animal
The Velveteen Rabbit
Gills Gone Wild
Wildlife
Petting Zoo
Pampered Pet
Pet Peeve
Unconditional Love

Arts/Crafts
(see also Talent)

Define & Design
Art from the Heart
Use Your Imagination
A Personal Touch
Imagine That
My True Colors
Perfectly Crafted
VIVID!
Masterpiece
Let's Chalk About It
Knitting Pretty
Beauty is in the Eye of the Beholder
On the Cutting Edge
A Work of Art
Express Yourself

Attitude/Ego

Me! Me! Me!
I'mperfection
SuperSize
Pride
Lip Service
What's Not to Like?
Simply Irresistible
All Me. All the Time.
Who's the Boss?
I ALWAYS Get What I Want
It's My Way or the Highway
Warning: Attitude at High Voltage
COCKY

Aunt
(see Family/Heritage)

Babysitting

Babyrunning
One Small Child; One Big Responsibility
It's A Dirty Job Butt Somebody's Gotta Do It
You've Got the Cutest Little Baby Face
It's a Small, Small World
Baby, You're the Best!
Trustworthy
Zoo Keeper
Oh, Baby!

Band/Musical Instruments
(See also Music and Talent)
Strike Up the Band
Band of Brothers
The Entertainer
BandStand
I'm with the Band
House Band
The Bassment
Making the Band
Sound the Trumpets
Battle of the Bands
Consistent C
Drummer Boy
Bang! Clash! Bang!
Ebony & Ivory

Baseball
(See also Sports/Games and Talent)
Play Ball!
bATTITUDE
Batter Up!
Hit and Run
Spring Fever
Who's on First?
Batman
SLUGGER
Spring Training
Play Brawl!
The Home Stretch
Diamonds are a Guys Best Friend
Take Me Out to the Ballgame
America's Favorite Pastime

Covering All the Bases
Foul Play

Basketball
(see also Sports/Games and Talent)

A Shooting Star
Basketbrawl
Ball Up
Hoops
Foul Play
Bricklayer
WHOOSH!
Hoopin' It
Big Shot
Hot Shot
Hoop Dreams
He Shoots! He Scores!
NBA Trainee

Beach
(see also Swimming/Water Sports)

Makin' Waves
Beauty and the Beach
Three by the Sea
The Sands of Time
From Sea to Shining Sea
Sand Man
Beach Bum
Beach Babes
FantaSea
Beach Bash

Surf's Up!
H2Oh!
A Shore Thing
Blue Crush
Sea of Love

Beauty

American Beauty
God's Wonder
A Perfect Ten
As Pretty as a Picture
Good Looks Run in the Family
Beauty, Joy, Grace
The Gift of Beauty
A Classic Beauty
Pure
Elegance
Beauty is in the Eye of the Beholder
Simply Stunning

Bedroom

Room Raiders
Make Room
Interior Design
Room to Grow
Cribs
Keep Out!
Come In
What a Mess!
Wall to Wall
Bed Head

The Write TEEN Words

Titles

Trading Spaces
Room Sweet Room
Contents Under Pressure
Sweet Dreams
My Dream Room
Enter at Your Own Risk
Airing the Dirty Laundry
There Used to be a Floor Here
Tornado Site
Room for Improvement
A Space of My Own
Room for One
Room to Breathe
Chat Room

Birthday
(see also Gift and Party)

I Wish...
Happy Birthday to Me!
Aged to Perfection
The Age of Innocence?
I'll Have My Cake and Eat It Too
Birthday Blues
Birthday Bash
Sweet Sixteen
Fifteen Candles
The In-BeTWEEN Years
The Birthday Girl
MY Day
Older, Better and Cuter

Books

Bookin' It
A Novel Idea
Bookworm
A Real Page Turner
And So the Story Begins...
Never Judge a Book by Its Cover
Use Your Imagination
An Open Book
Bookends

Bowling

As Sharp as a Bowling Ball
A Striking Performance
Get Your Mind Out of the Gutter
Bowled Over
Oh, Spare Me!
Bustin' Pins
SuperBowl

Boxing/Fighting
(see also Sports/Games and Talent)

It's 'Bout Time
TKO
The Contender
Roll with the Punches
Fight Club
Down for the Count
The Fist of Fury
Tough Enough
Keep Your Eye on the Prize

Fight Night
Bookends

Boyfriend
(See Dating and Love)

Boys
(See also Teenager)

Boys Will Be Boys
Man of Mystery
It's a Guy Thing
Boy Meets World
No Girls Allowed
From Dirt to Denim
Rough Around the Edges
Young Man
All Boy
Boy, Oh Boy!
Macho Man
Rugged Good Looks
A Jack-of-All-Trades
The Bachelor
Prince Charming
Boy Toy
Manly Man
Bad Boy
A Good Man is Hard to Find
Nice Guys Always Finish Last
The Bigger the Boy, the More Expensive the Toy
Boy Wonder
Tough Guy
Always a Gentleman
Unnecessary Roughness

The Joy of Boys
The Boys of Summer

Braces

EmBRACE the pain
The Silver Lining
BraceFace
A Shining Star

Break-up
(see also Friends-long distance and Memories)

The One that Got Away
Next!
I Miss You and Me
Don't Go Away Mad. Just Go Away.
A Change of Heart
The End.
c-ya!
On a Break
The Heartbreak Kid
He Loves Me, He Loves Me Not
Was It Something I said?
Out with the Old, In with the New
Heartbreaking
It's So Hard to Say Good-bye
Let's Kiss and Make Up
It is SO Over!
Available
Love Hurts
Time Heals
Dissed & Dismissed

Good-Bye & Good Riddance
The Ex-Factor

Brother
(see also Family/Heritage and Sibling)

Oh, Brother!
Brothers Since the Beginning, Friends 'Til the End
What's A Big Brother For?
Big Brother is Watching You
My Brother's Keeper
There's No Buddy Like You
Band of Brothers
Just Like My Brother
Brotherly Love
Bro'
Friends Since Day One
Oh, Bother!
He Did It
Brotherhood
Brother to Brother
Only a Brother Can Understand

Camping
(see also Nature and Off-road)

Roughing It
Happy Campers
What Was That Noise?
Roughin' It Easily
S'More Good Times
Survival of the Fittest
Always be Prepared

Wood You Like to Camp?
Keep Away from Flame
Welcome to Camp Wearebored
Oh, Starry Night

Car/Driving

Driven
Stretch the Limits
Always Going the Extra Mile
Hot Wheels
Road Warrior
Carsick
Washed Up
Experienced Drivers Only
My Way or the Highway
Driver's Ed Teacher: Dad
Put to the Test
Licensed to Drive
A Boy and His Toy
When You Wish Upon a Car...
Caution: Teenager Behind the Wheel
No Slowing Down
A Classic Beauty
Out and About
A Key Exchange
Road Crew
New Wheels
What a Wreck!
Curb Appeal
No Direction In Life
Gentlemen, Start Your Engines!
The Bigger the Boy, the More Expensive the Toy
The Wheel Deal

Titles

Built for Speed
A Little Dirt Never Hurt Anybody
Let's Bounce
Road Rules
Zero to Sixty
Full Throttle
Pimp My Ride
Life in the Fast Lane
A Need for Speed
Down the Road...

Cat
(See also Animal/Pet)

Catwoman
Fabulous Feline
Feline Fury
Nine Lives
Catastrophic
Copy Cat
Cats are People Too
Here Kitty, Kitty!
Scaredy Cat
Purrfect
MEOW
Kitten Smitten
One Cool Cat
The Dog Did It!
Nine Lives
Look What the Cat Dragged In

Character/Personality Traits
(See also Attitude, Beauty, Ego and Fun/Silliness)

I Am What I Am
Getting Personal
One-of-a-Kind
Uncensored
Charmed
Girly Girl
Yes, I Can.
Keeping It Real
The Sweetest Thing
Always a Gentleman
To Be Perfectly Honest
What I Like About You
To Know Me is to Love Me
Rough Around the Edges
Wild Thang
The Leader of the Pack
Don't Be Shy
All That
Happy-Go-Lucky
A Shining Star
The Sensitive Type
Ambitious
An Original
The Softer Side
Flirt Alert
Being Me
The Real Deal

Cheerleading
(see also Gymnastics, Sports/Games and Talent)

Athletic Supporter
Cheerleading is an Attitude
Go! Fight! Win!
Short Skirts and Attitude
How High Can You Go?
Team Spirit
Uplifting
Humble Tumbles
Tumble Trouble
Angel in the Air
Flirty Skirts
Cheerful
SPIRIT

Child
(see Teenager)

Chores

Life is a Chore
Do It & Do It Again
Such a Chore; Such a Bore
Cruel and Unusual Punishment
Slave for You
Good Housekeeping
A Labor of Love

The Write TEEN Words

Christmas
(see also Gift and Tradition)

Wish List
Christmas Princess
The Bigger the Boy, the More Expensive the Toy
O' Christmas Tree
Holidaze
Santa CAUSE
Ho! Ho! Ho!
Ho! Ho! Oh!
A Christmas Story
My Christmas Angel
All I Want for Christmas is...
Christmas Done Bright
A Holiday Home
Christmas Love
It's Beginning to Look a Lot like Christmas
Naughty or Nice?
Ornamental
SCROOGE
All Hearts Come Home for Christmas
'Twas the Night Before Christmas
Bah-Humbug!

Titles

Clothes
(see Shopping and Style)

Clubs/Committee/Leadership
(see also Talent)

The Campaign Trail
Follow the Leader
Itty Bitty Committee
Join the Club

Titles

Head of the Class
Vision Impossible
A Rebel with a Cause
Vote for Me
Vote for Pedro
Power Play
Committed

College
(see also Independence and School)

To Be or Not to Be
College Dropout
College Bound
Dorm Sweet Dorm
To the First Degree
Far from Home
College or Bust
College Knowledge
Campus Crusade
Kollege Bound

Computer

www.
Cyber Surf
FYI
Connecting...
Computer Bug
High Tech
World Wild Web
Virtually Best Friends
The World at My fingertips

The Computer Generation
High-Tech Red-Neck
You've Got Mail
A Monitored Life
CUOL
she-mail
e-male
Googled
hmwrk

Cousin
(see Family/Heritage)

Dance
(see also Music and Talent)
Into Your Arms
Wanna Dance?
Dance with Me
On Your Toes
Let Your Heart Guide
Dance Like Nobody's Watching
Dancing Your Way into Hearts
Dancing Duo
RadioActive
The Entertainer
Twinkle Toes
Sidekicks
Dancin' to a Different Beat

Dating
(see also Love)

Beauty and the Beast
The Beauty and the Geek
Make a Wish
Boy Meets Girl
Mr. Right (now)
Cute Couple
The Odd Couple
Committed
Opposites Attract
The Dating Game
He's a Boy; He's a Friend.
Parental Control
It's a Date!
The Bachelor
CRUSH
Player
Boy, Oh Boyfriend!
The First Kiss is the Sweetest
Out with the Old, In with the New
I ALWAYS Get What I Want
How Did it Get So Late So Early?
Kiss and Make Out
Play Date
The Man of My Dreams
A Dream Come True
Teen Fling
The Thrill of the Hunt
A True Romantic
Mine, All Mine
So Far, So Good
Forever Your Girl

Daughter
(see also Family/Heritage, Girl, and Teenager)

A Daughter is a Reflection of Her Mother's Heart
A Daughter is a Mother's Best Friend
I'm a Big Girl Now
From Bows to Boys
Like Mother, Like Daughter
Lifelong Friend and Daughter
A Daughter is Heaven on Earth
Ribbon Memories
Our Heart and Soul
My Daughter, My Hero
Connect the Daughters
Daddy's Little Angel?
Little Girl Lost
From Little Girl to Alien
A Daughter is Love
Dear Daughter,
Daddy's Girl

Diet

Lighten Up
Loser!
Fit Club
Weighting Anxiously
Weigh to Go!
Eat Now, Diet Later
Through Thick or Thin
You Are What You Eat
Fit and Fabulous
Livin' Large
Think Thin

Discipline/Grounding
(see Trouble)

Dog
(see also Animal/Pet)

Off the Leash!
The Ruff Life
All Dogs Go To Heaven
Peppy Dog
Pampered Pooch
Snakes and Snails and Puppy Dog Tails
Puppy Love
Man's Best Friend
Dog Days of Summer
Mutt's Wrong?
Dog Daze
Good Dog
One Howl of a Dog
It's a Dog's Life
Doggone Adorable
Puppy Play
Top Dog

Do-it-yourself/Handiwork
(see also Arts/Crafts and Talent)

Before and After
In a Fix
Mr. Fix-it
Do-it-herself
From the Ground Up
A Jack-of-All-Trades
Can I Build It? Yes, I Can!
A Work in Progress

Room for Improvement
Power Project
Man-made
Some Assembly Required
What a Difference
Home Improvement
Caution: Teenager at Work

Drama/School Program
(see also Talent)

It's Showtime!
Drama Queen
Oh, The Drama!
Act I
A Shining Star
Break a Leg!
A Real Character
Home Theater
The Star Treatment
A Falling Star
Behind the Scenes

Dreams/Goals/Ambition

Hitch Your Wagon to a Star
Believe...
Follow Your Bliss
You Can Do It
What If...
Follow Your Rainbow
The Prince of Dreams
Endless Possibilities

Titles

Daydream Believer
Vision Impossible
You Wish!
Dream It. Believe It. Achieve It.
Ambitious
You Goal Girl!
Living the Dream
I Have a Vision

Easter
(see also Tradition)

Sunrise Surprise
My Peeps
Eggstrordinary
He is Risen
The Hunt is On
Chick This Out!
Hoppy Easter
Simply to Dye For!

Exchange Student
(see also Friends-long distance)

Trading Spaces
Worlds Apart
Exchange Gifts
Mi Casa es tu Casa
The New Kid in Town

Excitement/Extreme Sports/Fear

Look Before You Leap
One Giant Leap for Mankind
Fear Factor
Ready, Set, NO!
A Death Defying Stunt
It's a Bird! It's a Plane! It's...
Maximum Velocity
Survivor
Life on the Edge
Jump Into Action
What Goes Up Must Come Down
Trust Me
The Sky's the Limit

Exercise/Physique

Don't Sweat It!
SuperSize
Girly Man
The Long and Short of It
Firm, Fit and Fabulous
Feel the Burn
Healthy Diet, Mind, Body and Lifestyle

Face
(See also Beauty)

Porefection
A Breakout Performance
Fabulash
Easy on the Eyes

Titles

Unforgettable
The Look of Love
The Ear-ly Years
The Eyes Have It
Smile Style

Family/Heritage

All in the Family
Family Feud
A Tree Full of Nuts
Family Matters
We Put the Fun in Dysfunctional
Ancestrally Challenged
It's All Relative
Set an Example
Past, Present and Our Future
Aunt She the Best?
Being an Aunt Means...
Dozens of Cousins
Loving Cousins
Monkey's Uncle
The Black Sheep of the Family
Good Looks Run in the Family
Through Good Times & Bad
It's in the Genes
GENERATIONS
Through the Years
The More the Merrier
From Generation to Generation
It All Starts and Ends with Family
A Heir Raising Experience
The Heart of the Home
Our Legacy
Family Values

Father
(see also Family/Heritage and Parent)

Who's Your Daddy?
Family Man
My Hero
Family Guy
The King Reigns
Like Father, Like Son
Daddy's Home
My Heart Belongs to Daddy
Father Along
A Father's Love
Big Daddy
Father Knows Best
The Man in the Middle
Guidance
The Ol' Man
Fatherhood
In Dad We Trust
Superman
Being a Father Means...
Strong Man, Gentle Heart

Fishing
(see also Swimming/Water Sports)

The Catch of the Day
Weapon of Bass Destruction
The Lure of Nature
The One that Got Away
Fishing for Compliments
Nice Catch
The Reel Deal

Football
(see also Sports/Games and Talent)

Friday Night Lights
Footbrawl
Touchdown!
NFL Trainee
The End Zone
In the Zone
Gridiron Guys

Friends/Best Friend
(see also Multiples)

Together Wherever
Side by Side
Sidekicks
Tight
Opposites Attract
Unique Unity
Friend or Foe?
Homeboy
BFF
To Know Her is to Love Her
What Are Friends For?
Partners in Crime
Dumb & Dumber
FUN-duh-MENTAL Friends
Gossip Gurus
Friendship in Bloom
The Best of Friends, The Best of Times
My Circle of Friends, Let It Never Be Broken
Bestest Buddies
The Gang
The More the Merrier
Friends 'Til the End

Inseparable
Me & My Shadow

Friends-long distance

Always Connected
It's Hard to Say Good-bye
The Road Between Friends is Short
The Long Good-bye
Close in Heart
So Far, So Good
Stay
Separate Paths
Together in Spirit

Fun/Silliness

Just For The Fun Of It
CRAZED
Uncensored
Wild Child
Just for Kicks
FUN-duh-MENTAL Friends
Crazy Daze
The Odd Couple
Why Be Normal?
Laughter is the Best Medicine
Giggle Giggle Giggle
Dumb & Dumber
Punk'd
LOL
Unraveled
Fun & Games
Good Times

Smile Style
Off the Hook
Good Times

Games
(see Sports/Games)

Gift
The Past and the Presents
I Want Your Presence
It's in the Bag
Bag Lady
Gifted
Thank You
TYVM
You REALLY Shouldn't Have
Big Things Come in Small Packages
It's Better to Give than to Receive
The Greatest Gift
Under Wraps
Wrapped in Love

Girls
(see also Teenager)
Teen Queen
Goddess
Girls Just Wanna Have Fun
Sugar and Spice and Everything Nice...
Thank Heaven for Teenage Girls
A Girl of Grace
Girl Power

Titles

Princess
Golden Girls
Brunette Babes
Drama Queen
Glamour Girl
It's a Girl Thing
Young Lady
Girls Rule
Uptown Girl
A Living Doll
Girls' Night Out
Girls Gone Wild
Lady in Training
Daddy's Girl
Pure Girl
She's All That
Girly Girl
Princess Diaries
Girls Will Be Girls
DIVA
Divine Divas
Girl Talk

Girlfriend
(see Dating and Love)

Glasses/Contacts
(also available: Sunglasses)

Eye Love You
An Eye-opening Experience
Avoid Contact with Eyes
Vision Impossible
Fabulash!

BCNU
Love at First Sight
Seeing Double
I Have a Vision
Focus

Golf
(see also Sports/Games and Talent)

Teed Off
FORE!
Par for the Course
In the Swing of Things
Foresight
A TEErific Sport
Staying the Course

Graduation
(see also Dreams/Goals/Ambition)

Commencement
No Looking Back
Looking Back, Moving Forward
Congrats!
College Bound
FINALLY
Into the Real World
The Future is Bright
Free at Last!
Outta Here!
Hats Off!
Edgicated
Now What?

The Graduate
The Scholar
Bye Senior High
The End.

Grandchild/Grandparent
(see also Family/Heritage)

An Antique
A Classic
A Living Legacy
My Hero
GRAND
Timeless Beauty
Spoiled by You-know-who
Everything Tastes Better at Grandma's House
Grandparents are Angles in Disguise
They Don't Call 'Em Grand for Nothing
Priceless Days
Wisdom
Been There, Done That
Nobody Grander

Growing Up
(see also Independence)

There Goes My Baby
A Major Development
The Way Things Were
Time Flies
Short, Small, Big, Tall
Growing Pains
As Time Passes

Titles

Precious Inches, Priceless Memories
All Grown Up
Fast Forward
Big Baby
Grow For It!
Just My Size
Measuring Up
Off the Charts
When I Grow Up...
I'm a Big Kid Now
It's a Small, Small World
Ready! Set! Grow!

Gymnastics
(see also Sports/Games and Talent)

Head Over Heels
Raising the Bar
Roll Model
Things Are Looking Up
Tumbleweed
Loco-motion
Flip-Flop

Habit

A Creature of Habit
Habitual Offender
Old Habits are Hard to Break
Keep Away From Flame
Again & Again & Again
Here I Go Again
Irresistible

Hair

A Brush with Disaster
Hair I am!
The Mane Attraction
Blonde Ambition
Brunette Beauty
Black Beauty
InspiRED
A World of Curls
A Hair Raising Experience
In Touch with My Roots
Knotty but Nice
Hairlarious
It's All in Your Head
Bed Head
Been Hair, Done That
Lighten Up
A Short Cut
Simply to Dye For!
Change My Mind, Change My Color
A New Do

Half-sibling

Half-brothers, Full of Love
Half Full or Half Empty?
Wholehearted
Half & Half

Halloween

Hauntingly Hot
Fright Night

BOOtiful
Creatures of the Night
Things that Go Bump in the Night
Dressed to Kill
Ghoulfriends
Boy Meets Ghoul
Boo Who

Handicap
(see Hardship and Special Needs)

Hang-out/Special Place
A Special Place in My Heart
All Roads Lead to...
Out and About
Good Food, Good Music, Great Times, Great Friends
Anywhere But Home
Priceless Nights
The Teen Scene

Hanukkah
Shining Bright
Oh, Dreidel, Dreidel, Dreidel
The Magical Menorah
Eight Lights, Eight Nights
The Power of Light
Feast of Dedication

Happiness

Follow Your Bliss
Loving Life
Happy-Go-Lucky
The Good Things in Life
You are My Sunshine
Immeasurable Pleasure
Laughter is the Best Medicine
Happiness is...
Live. Love. Laugh.
Life On Cloud Nine
Celebrate

Hardship

Heartbreak
A Spirit Unbroken
My Guardian Angel
A Leap of Faith
T-N-T (tough & tender)
Life is Fragile...Handle with Prayer
Tough Times
It's Too Hard
It's Not Fair
Broken Spirit
No Regrets

Hobby/Collection

Look What I've Got
Mine. All Mine.
Keepsake
Favorite Pastime

Titles

Memories to Hold
A Rare Find
Hunt & Gather
Collection Connection
More than a Hobby...a Habit

Hockey
(see also Sports/Games and Talent)

You Goal Girl!
The Final Goal
Crunching Ice
Puck Your Best Foot Forward
Ice Wars
Access Denied
Hot on the Ice
Playing it Cool

Home

Cribs
Mi Casa es tu Casa
There's No Place Like Home
Love Makes a House a Home
Love Thy Neighbor
Home Sweet Home
Home Sweet Apartment
Home Improvement
House of Horror
Home Again
Be My Guest
Dream Home
On the Move

Curb Appeal
Homemade
Wall to Wall
Homely
Come in!
Sizing It Up
Trading Spaces
Good Housekeeping
Room for Improvement
Anywhere But Home
Built from the Ground Up
Great Things Come in Small Packages
Living the American Dream
A Place to Call Home
Come Home
Room to Grow
The Door is Always Open
Home Is Where the Heart Is

Home School
(See also School)

Home Sweet Home School
Home is Where the Heart is
Home is Where the School is
From the Comforts of Home
A Labor of Love
Homemade
Only the Best

Homecoming
A Happy Homecoming
Homecoming: Game Going
Our Time to Shine
School Spirit

Hope Chest
Full of Hope
I Wish I May, I Wish I Might…
Sweet Dreams are Made of This
Tucked Away
Timeless Treasure

Hug/Kiss
Heart to Heart
Sweet Lips
A Kiss is Just a Kiss
I'm Stuck On You
Cuddles & Kisses
Too Close for Comfort
All Wrapped Up in Each Other
A Random Act of Kindness
Love One Another
Irresistible
Embrace Life
In the Heat of the Moment
The First Kiss is the Sweetest
Lip Service
H&K
huggles
Kiss and Make Up

Kiss and Make Out
XOXO
Cuddle Buddies
Come Closer

Hunting
The Thrill of the Hunt
The Buck Stops Here
Wild Turkey
Duck!
Big Shot
On the Hunt
BULLSEYE
Sharp Shooter

Illness/Injury
That's Sick!
Take Care
Sick Chick
Road to Recovery
Share & Share Alike
The Casting Couch
Oh, Gimme a Break!
Survivor
Homesick
Laughter is the Best Medicine
The Power of Prayer
Life is Fragile…Handle with Prayer
A Picture of Health
Is there a Doctor in the House?
Catch the Fever!

EMERGENCY
Healing Words
Can I Help?
Health Crisis
Break a Leg!
Agony of DeFeet
Bodily Harm
A Freak Accident
Time Heals All Wounds
Trial & Error
Boo-Boo
Brace Yourself
Castaway
On the Cutting Edge
OUCH!

Independence
Wings
Miss Independence
Watch Out World, Here I Come!
All By Myself
On My Own
Self-dependent
It's My Life
I'm a Big Girl Now
It's Now or Never
I Can Do That
Who Needs Parents?

Independence Day
Miss America
God's Country

Born in the U.S.A.
Pride and Patriotism
American Idol
American Idle
Oh, Say, Have You Seen...
Miss Independence
American Beauty
Land of the Brave
FREEDOM
In God We Trust
All-American
An American Tradition
American Pride
Only in America

Job
(see Work)

Laziness
Creature of Comfort
SLACKER
American Idle
Cover Girl
Chillin
Zzzzzzz
Recharging
Couch Warmer
Son Up to Son Down
Sweet Dreams are Made of This
Undercover
Mr. Dreamy
Bed Rest

Titles

Life/EveryDay Moments

One Day at a Time
Loving Life
Living the Good Life
Livin' la Vida Loca
It's My Life
The Surreal Life
Just Another Day
Priceless Days
The Fabulous Life of...
Life As We Know It
Lessons Learned
Everyday
Life's a Mystery
It's the Little Things in Life
These are the Days to Remember
The School of Life
The Life I Live
Days of Our Lives
The Journey
True Life
The Real World
Wildlife
The Simple Life
Dear Diary,
Living the American Dream
The Good Things in Life
The Good Life
Just Another Day

Love
(see also Dating)

Show Me Some Love
Love Hurts

The Write TEEN Words

Today, Tomorrow, Always
My Promise to You
Love Makes the World Go Around
I Wish You Love
Live. Love. Laugh.
The Power of Love
With All My Heart
A Love Story
Puppy Love
Lovesick
Love Conquers All
Love at First Sight
The Look of Love
Young Love
He Loves Me, He Loves Me Not
A Lot Like Love
My One & Only
The Things We Do for Love
Together Forever

Make-up
Kiss and Make-up
A Fresh Coat of Paint
Mirror Image
Girly Girl
Let's Make-up
Glamour Girl
Beauty School
Cover Girl
About Face
Easy on the Eyes
Beauty is Only Skin Deep

Martial Arts
(see also Sports/Games and Talent)
Kicking and Screaming
Roll with the Punches
Just for Kicks
Kick Butt
Freestyle
Side-kicks
Fist of Fury
Self-defense

Memories
Thanks for the Memories
Unforgettable
Cherish the Memory
Memories in the Making
Remember When...
Priceless
Memory Lane
A Lifetime of Memories
Live, Love, Laugh...Remember
Memorable Moments
Reflections
Treasured Thoughts
I'll Never Forget the Time...
From Everyday Moments to Cherished Memories

Memory of a Loved One
(see also Memories)
It's so Hard to Say Good-bye
A Walk in the Clouds

Empty Arms
The Good Die Young
Forget-me-not
A Passing Angel
Always Loved, Never Forgotten
Keeping the Memory Alive
Touched by an Angel
Gone but Not Forgotten
In Loving Memory

Military
HERO
Letters Home
Land of the Brave
Military Man
Rank and File
United We Stand
...and Our Flag was Still There
Until They All Come Home
All-American
Duty Calls
The New Recruit
Dear Soldier, Thank you! Love, the USA
Send in the Troops
Brave of Heart
Salute!
Let's Stop the Fighting
A Few Good Men (U.S. Marines)
Ready, Willing, and Able (U.S. Army)
Wings of Victory (U.S. Air Force)
Above and Beyond (U.S. Air Force)
Proud to Serve (U.S. Navy)

The Write TEEN Words

Titles

Money
Pricele$$
Save Me!
Cha-Ching!
Rich in Friends
I Owe it All to You
Big Spender
Cash Flow
Dollars & Sense
Who Wants to be a Millionaire?
All About the Benjamins
A Priceless Friendship
SPENT

Mother
(see also Family/Heritage and Parent)
My Guardian Angel
All About Mom
Like Mother, Like Daughter
Unconditional Love
A Mother's Touch
Mother & Child
Working Mom
"Stay-at-home" Mom...Ha!
The Mother I Never Knew
A Mother's Work is Never Done
A Mother is a Girl's Best Friend
The Lady of the House
A Special Lady
My Hero
Momma
Yo Momma!
Mother Nurture
Motherhood

Momma Trauma
I Owe it All to you
A Mother's Love
The Motherload
Being a Mother Means...
Mother Knows Best

Motorcycle
Born to be Wild
Hog Heaven
Two Tired
The Cycle of Life
Biker Babe
Biker Buddies
Ride to Live. Live to Ride.

Movies/Television
Home Theater
Coming to a Screen Near You
Now Showing
Watch This
Couch Potato
Video Vixen
FANatic
As Seen on TV
The Reel World
A Real Character

Multiples
(see also Sibling)

Three's a Charm
Twice as Nice
Three Dimensional
Mirror Images
Double Your Pleasure
Double Trouble
Two Much Alike
Triple Trouble
Three of a Kind
Three's Company
Three's a Charm
Seeing Double
Another One?
Five Times the Fun
Copy Cats
Who's Who?
Split Personalities

Music
(see also Band/Musical Instruments and Talent)

Turn It Up!
VOLUME
You Rock!
IPod, Do You?
Living in Harmony
Under Raps
High Tech
MP3's a Charm
The Apple of My iPod
Let Your Heart Sing

RadioActive
The Sound of Music

Nature
(see also Off-road)

Natural Habitat
Park it!
Mountain Time
Treemendous Fun
It's Only Natural
The Great Outdoors
On the Lookout
A Force of Nature
Naturally...
The Scenic Route
Trail Blazer
Get Out!
Breathtaking
Go Play Outside
The Call of the Wild
Getting Back to Nature
Mother Nature

New Year

Resolutions
New Year Revolutions
In One Year and Out the Other
New Promises
The Future Looks Bright
Out with the Old, In with the New
Out with a Bang

Titles

The Year in Review
5! 4! 3! 2! 1...Happy New Year!

Off-Road
(see also Nature)

Off the Beaten Path
Monster Truck
Mud Buds
Down and Dirty
A Little Dirt Never Hurt Anybody
New Paths

Parade

On Parade
Parading Around
Floating By
Don't Rain on My Parade
A Big Production
An Annual Event

Parent
(see also Family/Heritage, Father, Mother, and Teenager)

Parental Control
Forces of Nature
Source of Embarrassment
Being the Parent of a Teenager Means...
It's a Dirty Job but Somebody's Gotta Do It

The Joys & Trials of Parenting a Teen
The Proud Parents
Married with Children
Parenthood
Unconditional Love
How Do You Do It?
Being a Parent Means...
Give & Take
24/7
An Heir Raising Experience
Great Expectations
Two Much Alike
Me & My Shadow

Parent/Child Relationship
(See Parent)

Party
Let's Get the Party Started
It's My Party and I'll Cry If I Want To
Party Animals
Bad Company
House Party
Party 'til the Sun Comes Up
The Life of the Party
The Party Planner
You're Invited
Party Girl
Let's Party!
It's Party Time!

Passover

Shining Bright
Freedom Festival
The Passover Spirit
The Season of Freedom
A Holy Week
Matzoh Meal

Prom
(see also Dance and Dating)

PROMise
A Moment Like This
Promparazzi
Simply Stunning
The PROMblem
My Beautiful Prom Mess
The Beauty and the Geek
From Geek to Glam
A Prominent Couple
Dress Stress
Dressed to Kill
Post Prom Party

Rock-Climbing
(see also Excitement/Extreme Sports/Fear)

Rock Star
Off the Wall
You Rock!
Climbing the Walls
Between a Rock and a Hard Place

Boulder & Beautiful
A Milestone
Rock Bottom

Running
(see also Sports/Games and Talent)
The Amazing Race
Hit the Ground Running
Build for Speed
The Agony of De-feet
Good Looks Run in the Family
The Fast Track
Beauty in Motion
One Track Mind
Life in the Fast Lane
On Your Mark! Get Set! Go!
Always Going the Extra Mile
Running Wild
Road Runner

School
A Class Act
Saved by the Bell
hmwrk
Study Buds
Stop, Look and Lesson
Lessons Learned
School Spirit
School Daze
Stud Study
Hittin' the Books

Titles

Too Cool for School
A Star Student
Edgication
Bus STOP!
Makin' the Grade
A Passing Interest
HisStory
It Doesn't Add Up
Bad Chemistry
Do You Speak English?
The School of Life
Scholarship Material
Teacher's Pet
Put to the Test

Scouts

Be Prepared
Scouts Honor
Scouting
Make New Friends
Dedication

Scrapbooking
(see also Arts/Crafts, Hobby/Collection and Memories)

The Pages of My Life
Saving Memories, Making New Ones
Past & Present for the Future
One Page at a Time
And the Story Begins...
Scrapaholic

Made with Love
All About Me
Cuttin' Up

Shopping
(see also Style)

Sale Away with Me
At All Costs
Swap Shop
Retail Therapy
Budget Buster
Sleep, Eat, School, Shop
Coming Soon to a Mall Near You
The Price is Right
A Cents of Style
Shopaholic
Shopping is in My Jeans
Spending Spree

Sibling
(see also Brother, Family/Heritage, Sister)

Double Trouble
Oh, Brother! It's My Sister!
A Shared Past
Déjà vu
Sibling Rivalry
Sibling Revelry
Sibling Secrets
Remember When We...
Inseparable

Titles

In the Middle of It All
Sibling Similarities
Built-in Friends
Partners in Crime

Sister
(see also Family/Heritage and Sibling)

Sisterhood
Sister to Sister
My Sister, My Friend
Sister, Sister
Twisted Sister
Sister Solidarity
A Sister's Love
She Did It
My Sister's Keeper
Sisters of the Heart
Sister Act
Sis Bliss
What are Big Sisters For?
Sisters Since the Beginning, Friends to the End
A Sister Understands

Skateboarding
(see also Excitement/Extreme Sports/Fear and Talent)

GR8 2 SK8
Rocket Power
Gliding Through life
Carving Concrete
Freestyle

Skating
(See also Excitement/Extreme Sports/Fear and Skateboarding)

Fire & Ice
Mountain Time
Head for the Hills
Cool
Uplifting
Crunching Ice
Dashing Through the Snow
Ice Princess
Iceman
Roller Derby
Slip 'N Slide
Hittin' the Slopes
Snow Bunny
Winter Wonderland
Hot on the Ice

Skiing
(See Skating)
(Water Skiing: See Swimming/Water Sports)

Sleepover
(See also Party)

Trading Spaces
Sleeping Beauties
Undercover
The Dream Team
SLEEPisOVER
While You Were Sleeping
Slumberless Party
No Rest for the Weary

The Queen & Her Princesses
Dreamy
Sleepy Heads
Bed Heads

Snow

Fire & Ice
Snow Buddy Else
Head for the Hills
Warmest Wishes
Ice Princess
Snow Angels
Snow Day
No Two Are Alike
A Child of All Seasons
If We Could Freeze Time...
Let It Snow, Let It Snow, Let It Snow
Dashing Through the Snow
The Snowball Fight Championship
The Weather Outside is Frightful
Frost Bites!
Be Cool
Chillin'

Soccer
(see also Sports/Games and Talent)

Soccer Brawl
A Goal in Life
You Goal Girl!
Hands Off!
Kickin' It

Access Denied
Kicking & Screaming
Put Your Best Foot Forward

Softball
(see also Baseball, Sports/Games and Talent)

Diamonds are a Girls Best Friend
Walk Softly but Carry a Big Stick
Hardcore Softball
Hit Like a Girl
Softbrawl
SOFTball? Hardly!
Diamond Divas

Son
(see also Boy, Family/Heritage and Teenager)

The Prodigal Son
The Rising Son
My Son, My Hero
A Sonny Outlook
Like Father, Like Son
The Young Man of the House
The Son that Brightens My Day
Lifelong Friend and Son
A Son is Love
He's Mine
My Son Shines
Sonsational!
Son of a Gun

Special Needs

Special Indeed
eSPECIALly NEEDed
A Spirit Unbroken
Special in So Many Ways
Especially Special
Perfect in Every Way

Sports/Games
(see also Excitement/Extreme Sports/Fear Talent and specific sports)

Power Play
Playing the Field
Dream Team
Game Day
Eat, Sleep, Play Ball
Good Clean Fun
Nice Guys Finish Last
Unnecessary Roughness
Boo-Yah!
An American Tradition
MVB (Most Valuable Benchwarmer)
Let the Games Begin!
Practice Makes Perfect
Practice Hard. Play Harder.
The Heart of a Champion
The Power Within
Winning Isn't Everything
The Agony of DeFeet
Tough Enough?
Girls Rule
Daddy's Athlete
Fun & Games
Pick a Card...Any Card...

Wild Card
Against All Odds
Card Shark
Poker Face
What's Your Deal?
Yeah, I bet!
Video Vixen
Playmates
In Our Defense
Team Rivalry
Born to Play
Ball Babe
The Girl's Got Game
The Belle of the Ball
The Rookie
Havin' a Ball
Play-by-Play
It Runs in the Family
ALL-STAR
MVP
Team Work
Teen Work
Outwit, Outplay, Outlast
Got Game?
On the Ball
CHAMP
Don't Sweat It!

Spring Break
(See also Travel)

On a Break
Give Me a Break!
Spring Fling
Spring Break-up

Titles

What Happens at Spring Break Stays at Spring Break
Spring Into Action
Teen Fling
Spring Fling

St. Patrick's Day
Leprechaun Day
Lucky Charm
St. Paddy's Day
Kiss Me, I'm Irish
Just My Luck
In a Pinch

Step-Parent/Step-Sibling
Married w/Children
Trading Spouses
The First Step
Father by Marriage, Daddy by Love
Welcome
The Heart of a Dad
My Other Mother
Stepping In
A Heart to Call Sister

Style
(see also Shopping)
In One Year and Out the Other
Dressed to Kill

The Write TEEN Words

Titles

What Not to Wear
Bling it on!
From Geek to Glam
Smile Style
Casual
Role "Model"
Mirror Image
Girly Girl
Accessory Necessity
Warning! Contents May be Hot!
How Do You Like Me Now?
Unraveled
Closet Case
GLAM
Express Yourself
On the Cutting Edge
It's In My Jeans
Glamour Girl
Where's the Dress Code When You Need One?
What's Your Style?
To Each His Own
One-of-a-Kind
The Look You Love
You're Out!
Stunning Style
You Are What You Wear

Summer

Scorchin'!
It's All About the Flip Flops
In the Heat of the Moment
Lazy Summer Daze
Summer Fun
That's Hot

Titles

Too Cool
Spring into Summer
Too Hot to Handle

Sunbathing
(see also Summer)

Some Like it Hot
Sunny Side Up
Sun Goddess
Toasted Buns
A Golden Glow
Red-faced
Suits Me!
Bikini Babes
Bathing Beauty
Sun-Kissed
Itty Bitty Teenie Weenie Bikini

Sunglasses

Cool Confidence
A Shady Character
Summer Shades

Surfing
(see Beach and Swimming/Water Sports)

Swimming/Water Sports
(See also Beach)

DIVErse
Take the Plunge
Blue Bound
In Over My Head
Row, Row, Row Your Boat
Get on Board
Dive In!
In the Swim of Things
The Talent Pool
Smooth Surfing
Wave Rider
The Pool Boy
Makin' a Splash
Pool Pals

Talent
(See also Dreams/Goals/Ambition)

Gifted
Practice, Practice, Practice
Practice Makes Perfect
Do You Have What it Takes?
Good, Really Good
Multi-talented
Talent Show
Talent Shown
Ready, Willing and Able
Good Looking and Talented Too
A Natural
It's in the Genes
Talented Teen
Super Powers
Bankable Talent

The Write TEEN Words

Titles

Tattoo/Piercing
(see also Style)

Every Body has a Story
There are Holes in Your Story
Self-Expression
Holey Cow!
Piercing my Heart
Branded
Inked
Body Art

Teenager
(see also Boy, Character/Personality Traits, Girl, Growing Up, Independence)

The Next Generation
A Work in Progress
Teen Fling
Adult in Progress
Diamond in the Rough
To Be Announced...
When I Grow Up...
You are What You Wear
Teen Spirit
Rookie
What Matters Most
The In BeTWEEN Years
I Know It All... I'm Already 16
Children are Angels with Crooked Halos
The Age of Innocence?
Today's Teenager
Wild Child
Whatever
Kiddin' Around

This Child of Mine
The Teen Scene
The Apprentice
Kids will be Kids
My Wish for You...
The Future
Child's Play
Spoiled Rotten
The World's Best Kid
Kool Kid

Telephone

Miss Information
Talk is NOT Cheap
Teenager for Cell; 45¢ per Minute
Telephone. Tell a Friend. Tell a Girl.
The Call of the Wild
Phone Home
Girl Talk
Look Who's Talking
Can You Hear Me Now?
Express Yourself
Express Your Cell
Free Speech
You Said It
Understated
Always a Phone Call Away
Who's Line is it Anyway?
Accessory Necessity
So Much for "Free" Speech!
Connecting

Tennis/Racquetball
(see also Sports/Games and Talent)

Love Means Nothing
Matchmakers
You Got Served
Racquet Science
Tennis Anyone?
In the Swing of Things

Thanksgiving
(see also Tradition)

A Time for Thanks
A Taste of Thanksgiving
An Abundance of Blessings
Thanks But No Thanks
Turkey Time
What a Turkey!
Thanks
So Thankful

Tradition

From Past to Present
Traditionally, We...
Generation to Generation
Tradition Transition
A Family Tradition
Here We Go Again
Same People, Same Place, Different Year
An Annual Event
Making Memories

Travel
(see also Car/Driving)

Take Me Away
Getting There is Half the Fun
Bon Voyage
The Sky's the Limit
New Paths
On the Fly
Goin' Places
World Travelers
So Far, So Good
The Road Between Friends is Short
No Direction in Life
The Great Escape
Wish You Were Here
Are We There Yet?
Get-away

Trouble

Guilty as Charged
I Plead the Fifth
Partners in Crime
Bad Company
Oops
Busted!
The Unusual Suspect
Double Trouble
Habitual Offender
How Did It Get So Late So Early?
Cruel and Unusual Punishment
Tempted by Temptation
Presumed Innocent
Grounded for Life

Titles

Trust Me!
The Scene of the Crime
The Black Sheep of the Family
What's the Worst that Could Happen?
Law & Order
The Outlaw
A Troubled Child
Don't Tell On Me
Uh-oh!

Uncle
(see Family/Heritage)

Vacation
(see Travel)

Valentine's Day
(see also Love)

Be Mine
Sweet Nothings
My Funny Valentine
Happy Heart Day
Romance Calls
You Hold My Heart
Cupid's Day

Volleyball
(see also Sports/Games and Talent)

Volleybrawl
Dig It!
In Your Face
Hit Like a Girl
Volley This!
You've Been Served

Volunteer Work

How Can I Help?
Making a Difference in the World
A Work of Heart
I Care
Touching Lives
Any Volunteers?
Do-gooders
A Labor of Love
A Personal Touch

Work
(see also Money)

Opportunity Knocks
Millionaire in Training
Would You Like to Supersize That?
Working for the Weekend
Dream Job vs. Reality
Who's the Boss?
Working Together
A Labor of Love
All Work. No Play.

Titles

You've Gotta Start Somewhere
Take This Job and...
It Takes Teen Work
Entrepreneur
Work It, Girl!
Caution: Teenager at Work
Mind Your Own Business
It's a Dirty Job But Somebody's Gotta Do It
Another Day, Another Dollar
Responsibility Sucks
The Apprentice
Help Wanted
Working Hard or Hardly Working?
I Owe! I Owe! So Off to Work I Go

Wrestling
(see also Sports/Games and Talent)

Smack Down
Show No Mercy
Let's Get Ready to Rumble!
Take it to the Mat

Yard Work
(see also Chores)

Curb Appeal
Lawn Ranger
Ready, Set, Mow
Grasshoppers
The Backyard Boys

Titles

Poetry is what in a poem makes you laugh,
cry, prickle, be silent,
makes your toe nails twinkle,
makes you want to do this or that or nothing,
makes you know that you are alone
in the unknown world,
that your bliss and suffering is forever shared
and forever all your own.
-Dylan Thomas

Poetry

Adoption/Foster Child
(see also Anguish/Despondency)

One of us, I'm proud to be
He, she, we, them and me,
This awesome family
Blended perfectly.
-Crystal Dawn Perry

Heartbroken child come live with me
Where your heart can mend and be free-
Free from pain and free to believe
Free to give love and free to receive.
-Crystal Dawn Perry

Amusement Park
(see Excitement/Extreme Sports/Fear)

Anguish/Despondency

I can't turn back the hands of time
Or change what has been done
I can't exchange the cards life dealt
Nor stop what has begun
At times I don't know what to say
I'm scared to show my heart
I'm sometimes awkward and confused
On how to play my part
But nothing that I say or do
Can give me the control
Of what was never in my hands
but battles with my soul.
-Jennifer R. Shaner

Where is my child that would cry in the night
And wouldn't stop 'til I held him tight?
At times he would say, "Mommy, I need you."
Maybe I didn't say it but I needed him too.
Where is my child that gave me sweet hugs?
My heartstrings long to feel that tug.
I loved him then as I love him now;
I want to reach him but I don't know how.
If you should pass him along life's path,
Tell him his mother needs him back.
-Crystal Dawn Perry

I'm surrounded by people
But I'm still all alone
I'm in my house
But I'm still lost
I'm in a wide-open field
But I feel trapped
I long to be free.
-Matt Horton

How sad one's life
When there's no hope.
When times are tough
Dreams help you cope.
Perhaps your dreams
Won't all come true
But trust there's some
You will see through.
So keep some hope.
Reach for the stars.
Embrace the chance.
The dreams can be ours.
-Jennifer R. Shaner

Animal/Pet

The times we've shared
I'll never forget
I'll love you forever-
My loyal pet.
-Crystal Dawn Perry

Tired and hungry
No place to call home
Scared and lonely
In the streets you roamed
My heart is shared
It's no longer my own
It's where you live now
We'll never be alone.
-Crystal Dawn Perry

Playing, running,
Licked me again
Priceless moments
With my fuzzy friend.
-Crystal Dawn Perry

Arts/Crafts
(see also Talent)

The beauty of the craft that I create
Can be expressive of love or expressions of hate
My skill gives me hope, completion and power
It's the light of life in my darkest hour
In hopes that my work will be a treasure
For the mood of my heart is my craft's measure.
-Crystal Dawn Perry

Attitude/Ego

My wish for you
Is a new attitude...
Laughing, crazy
Smiling and cool.
-Crystal Dawn Perry

What else is there?
It's not hard to see;
That what is important
Is all about me!
-Crystal Dawn Perry

Said with attitude
Meant to be cool
So you think it's rude,
"Whatever, Dude!"
-Crystal Dawn Perry

Aunt
(See Family/Heritage)

Babysitting

I'm honored to be trusted
With your child's well-being
His tantrums, his spills
His random pee-ing.
I know this hard work
Will make me stronger
And teach me to put off
Parenthood longer.
-Crystal Dawn Perry

I'm off to catch a running nose.
Now what's that smell? Sure not a rose!
I feed you as you slobber and slurp.
I look into your eyes. You let out a burp.
Then a smile...you're charming and sweet.
Babysitting you can be a treat.
-Crystal Dawn Perry

10 perfect fingers and 10 perfect toes
Mommy's eyes and Daddy's nose
A wonderful miracle from heaven above
Oh, little baby, how much you are loved!
-Dana Roberts Clark

Band/Musical Instruments
(see also Music and Talent)

Standing tall, instrument in hand,
Making sure to reach the mark
Staying in step, sounding out,
Inspiring crowds as we march.
-Crystal Dawn Perry

The stands are scattered
With members of the band
Friends meeting friends
And loyal fans

There for support
at an unpleasant end
Or singing the praises
Of their team in a win.
-Crystal Dawn Perry

Baseball
(See also Sports/Games and Talent)

Boys taking a swing at life
And the American tradition
Running after soaring dreams
To catch their ambitions.
-Crystal Dawn Perry

The players on the field yell,
"Swing! Batter! Batter!"
The fans in the bleachers
Start to swelter.
The air smells
Of hotdogs and dirt.
The bat swings
And the crowd goes berserk!
-Crystal Dawn Perry

Basketball
(See also Sports/Games and Talent)

Dribble. Pass.
Shoot. Score.
Up again
For two more.
-Crystal Dawn Perry

Through the air
Never falling short...
A shooting star
On the basketball court.
-Crystal Dawn Perry

Beach
(see also Swimming/Water Sports)

Trees grab the wind and hold its song,
Ocean music plays on and on.
Gentle kisses of airborne sea,
Dance on the waves and call to me.
-T.R. Cardinet

Seagulls, blue sky,
Crashing waves,
Footprints, cares...
Drifting away.
-Crystal Dawn Perry

Beauty

You are an undeniable beauty,
The world warmed by your radiance.
Your eyes sparkle and intrigue.
Your smile brightens and enchants.
Watching your beauty, inside and out
I say, "Thank you, My Dear,
You have taught my soul to dance."
-Crystal Dawn Perry

Bedroom

A home as her castle
A bed for her throne
Her quest for asylum
And the royal phone
Friends as jesters
Or studying alone
The Princess rules court
In a room of her own.
-Crystal Dawn Perry

I wish that my room had a floor!
I don't so much care for a door,
But this crawling around
Without touching the ground
Is getting to be quite a bore!
-Gelett Burgess

Birthday
(See also Gift and Party)

I have new dreams
I've conquered fears
I've laugh with friends
They've dried my tears
I've blushed at jokes
I've cried at sneers...
The future and past
Of another year.
-Crystal Dawn Perry

Time to celebrate again
With tasty treats to share
Bright boxes on the table
More presents on a chair
One more candle on the cake
To mark another year,
But the greatest gift of all
Is having loved ones near.
-Jennifer R. Shaner

The best parts of birthdays
Are presents and friends
And memories made
To be shared again.
-Crystal Dawn Perry

Books

Open the paper door.
Enter a world that unfolds.
Lost in thoughts, deep yet not dark,
The story has been told.
-Crystal Dawn Perry

Bowling

One day you'll see me
On E.S.P.N.
Then you can say,
"I knew him when..."
-Crystal Dawn Perry

Rarely a strike
Possibly a spare
At least once
In the gutter.

It must be the ball
Or the wrong shoe size...
Or else
I would have done better!
-Crystal Dawn Perry

Boxing/Fighting
(See also Sports/Games and Talent)

A jab from the left
Uppercut with the right
Let it be said,
"He fought the good fight."
-Crystal Dawn Perry

They step in the ring
(Though I swear it looks square)
Anxiety, excitement,
The smell of sweat in the air
The ref starts the bout
A circular dance abounds
A couple of punches
The end of that round
Letting off steam
Adrenaline ignites
Moms and friends pray
For a good end to the fight.
-Crystal Dawn Perry

Boyfriend
(See Dating and Love)

Boys
(See also Teenager)

Sports, Tennis Shoes,
Girls & Hair Issues
Sleeping Late, Naps
and Baseball Caps...
This is what big boys are made of.
-Crystal Dawn Perry

When God made a girl,
He gave her beautiful hair
And perfect lips.

When God made a boy
With ragged hair and big feet-
His hand must've slipped.
-Crystal Dawn Perry

Strong when you need to be,
Tough when you have to be,
Gentle when you should be;
You're everything to me.
-Crystal Dawn Perry

Braces

Brace yourself
For what you will see-
A mouth full of silver
Enhancing me

So bright and dazzling
One can hardly see
But that's not braces-
It's personality!
-Crystal Dawn Perry

Mouth full of metal
Oh! How it aches
Soup and more soup
Is all I ate.
-Andrea Clark

Break-up

Remember those laughs we'd share together
Dreaming of life we'd share forever
Remember that smile you used to give
Seeing it gave me reason to live
Remember those times you'd hold me tight
Being close to your body felt so right
Remember those tears we finally cried
Knowing our time together had died
Remember these words I say to you...
As long as I live, my love for you is true.
-Katie Leigh Taylor

Too many days I've missed your smile
Without you my heart's torn
You come to me in nightly dreams
But vanish with the morn
I hope you'll soon return to me
And then my heart will mend
I need the shelter of your arms
My life, my love, my friend.
-Jennifer R. Shaner

Sometimes we're cool.
Sometimes we're hot.
Sometimes we're together.
Sometimes we're not.
-Crystal Dawn Perry

Brother
(See also Family/Heritage and Sibling)

Think of our fights,
One after another,
As my way of saying,
"I love you, brother."
-Crystal Dawn Perry

Apart, together,
Nearer or farther,
You'll always be
My big bother.
-Crystal Dawn Perry

Thank you for being there
When I need a friend.
You are the best brother
No matter where or when.
-Suzan L. Wiener

He has slugged me
He has hugged me
He has hated me
He has loved me
Seen my good side
Seen my bad
Told our Mom
Sided with Dad
He broke my heart
He made me laugh
My brother always,
My friend, at last.
-Crystal Dawn Perry

Camping

Camping out beneath the stars
Ghost stories by the fire
Crickets play soft lullabies
Backed by a frog led choir
Hot dogs roasted over flames
A nice end to the week
Wait...I felt a drop of rain
I hope the tent won't leak!
-Jennifer R. Shaner

Camping under starry skies
Or splashing in the pool
Time to laugh and hang with friends
But best of all- no school!
-Jennifer R. Shaner

Car/Driving

Fender benders, dents, broken glass, whiplash;
It's easy to see why they call me "Crash."
-Crystal Dawn Perry

Red means stop. Green means go.
I tried to teach you all that I know.
Now that you're behind the wheel,
Before my Father I will kneel.
I pray that He will keep you safe.
Please, be careful, for everyone's sake.
-Dana Roberts Clark

Traveling the roads near and far
Showing off my own car.
A lucky few can ride with me
All others must walk with envy.
-Crystal Dawn Perry

As you run in the yard, I watch from the window
Your cheeks are rosy, your hair in a bow
You're smile is as bright as morning sun
I'm grateful for this life that has just begun.
Then I'm startled when I hear a car start
Tears of joy now burn with ache in my heart
You sit behind the wheel. You're nearly grown.
How could it be that the time has flown?
You were my baby and always will be
I whisper, "I love you"
As you drive away from me.
-Crystal Dawn Perry

I studied the book a hundred times.
I know the signals and the names of the signs.
I practiced driving every chance I got.
Now I have a license to keep the roads hot!
-Crystal Dawn Perry

Grab the keys
There's no time to spare
The mall is open
I've got to get there!
-Crystal Dawn Perry

"I need a job", I heard you say
"To pay my bills and my own way."
So now with money, here you are-
Dressed to a tee and with your own car.
-Margo Dill

Cat
(see also Animal/Pet)

Here are the rules,
Let it be said:
I will make demands
But I do not beg.
Read my mind
When I rub your leg.
Unless you are ordered,
Don't rub my head.
Don't laugh when I fall
From the window ledge.
Though I own the house
I'll share the bed-
I get the pillow.
You get the edge.
-Crystal Dawn Perry

Rule #1:
I am the cat.
I rule the house
And that is that!
-Crystal Dawn Perry

Character/Personality Traits
(see also Beauty)

Intelligence and spirit
A sweet and gentle soul
Laughter chasing cares away
Smiles that makes me whole.
-Jennifer R. Shaner

With a brilliant mind
And your acts so kind
Thoughtful and smart...
Love grows in your heart.
-Crystal Dawn Perry

You should walk with pride
With your head held high.
You should talk as though
You have nothing to hide.
There is no reason not to,
Yet you are so shy.
Let them see what I see-
Let them see you shine.
-Crystal Dawn Perry

To lessen your stress,
I have the key:
Take life as it is
And live it carefree.
-Crystal Dawn Perry

Joy, Elation, Happiness,
Delight, Pleasure, Gladness
Cheerfulness, Bliss-
You give more than all this.
-Crystal Dawn Perry

Cheerleading
(see also Sports/Games, Gymnastics, and Talent)

Cheering for our team,
We dance and make a rumble.
We fly through the air,
Do toe-touches and tumble.
-Amber D. Clark

We've come to cheer
But we're bound to flirt
'Cause we look so good
In our little skirts.
-Crystal Dawn Perry

Scream, smile, jump and cheer
Fly thorough the air with no fear
Standing out in a crowd
Looking good, being loud.
-Crystal Dawn Perry

Child
(see Teenager)

Chores

Work, work, work-
It's such a bore.
At times, life feels like
One big chore.
-Crystal Dawn Perry

The lazy days of summer
The grass continues to grow
No chance for me to be lazy
Once again, I have to mow.
-Crystal Dawn Perry

Christmas
(see also Gift and Tradition)

My heart fills with wishes
And dreams to come true
Of spending Christmas
And the New Year with you.
-Crystal Dawn Perry

Ornaments that sparkle
And old ones discolored
Kindergarten bric-a-brac
Newly discovered.
-Crystal Dawn Perry

Santa Claus still visits me
As I sleep on Christmas Eve.
When it comes to getting gifts-
Of course I still believe!
-Crystal Dawn Perry

Christmas is
The time of year
When the past is behind us
And loves ones are near.
-Crystal Dawn Perry

Clothes
(see Shopping and Style)

Clubs/Committee/Leadership
(see also Talent)

A club is...
Students together
Making life more fun
And school better.
-Crystal Dawn Perry

I've got what it takes-
Hope and ambition
So trust me to succeed
In my promising mission.
I'll be your hope,
Your warrior and voice
Doing justice to the role
Of a leader's position.
-Crystal Dawn Perry

Passion or obsession,
Call it what you will.
It's something I must do.
I must excel!
-Crystal Dawn Perry

College
(see also Independence and School)

It's off to higher learning
In search of a degree
Needing skills for a career
Still learning about me
Good-bye to high school days
And friends I leave behind
Ahead awaits adventure
Where dreams are mine to find.
-Jennifer R. Shaner

Computer

I stare at the screen
For hours on end
I should be studying
But I'm chatting with friends.
-Crystal Dawn Perry

Bytes, chips, download, boot,
Edit, copy, paste, reboot
Memory, computer, application,
Cursor, keyboard, calibration
Program, CD, floppy disk
Hard drive, mouse, monitor, bits
Logging on, website, scan,
e-mail, virus, save, send
RAM, ROM, format, screen
All this makes me want to scream!
-Crystal Dawn Perry

I'm quite a sight to see
For at the end of my fingers are keys,
My face seems stuck, my eyes are glazed
And I can't move away from the screen.
-Crystal Dawn Perry

Cousin
(See Family/Heritage)

Dance
(See also Music and Talent)

Dance like this day was made for you
As though the earth stands still when you do
Don't say a word. Just close your eyes.
Listen to the music and let your heart guide
Believing everything you are is enough
As you dance to the tune of life.
-Crystal Dawn Perry

Hand in hand,
Taking a chance
On finding love
At tonight's school dance.
-Crystal Dawn Perry

Take me in your arms
Near your pounding heart
Tell me it beats for me
And we'll never be apart.
-Crystal Dawn Perry

Dating
(see also Love)

Will he ask? Will he call?
Should I wait by the phone
Or go ahead to the mall?
I hope...I pray...I dare to dream
That he'll ask me out-
If not, I will scream!
-Crystal Dawn Perry

Nervous glances and first sweet kiss
Long hours on the phone
Excitement every time we meet
New love to call my own.
-Jennifer R. Shaner

Let your heart guide.
Trust what feels right.
Forget all tomorrows
Tonight is our night.
-Crystal Dawn Perry

Shy but smiling glances
Nervous butterflies
Waiting for that moment...
Answers in his eyes
-Jennifer R. Shaner

Daughter
(see also Family/Heritage, Girls and teenager)

My precious daughter, growing fast
Such beauty lives within
Some days life's journey will be tough
But I know you will win
Your lovely smile can light a room
Your laughter clears the skies
I see courage in your spirit
There's kindness in your eyes
There may be days I will forget
To say how much I care
But always know you make me proud
Forever I'll be there.
-Jennifer R. Shaner

There were times when I thought you didn't care
But now I can see you were always there.
Some of your actions I didn't understand.
I admit I resented your upper hand.
You were doing what you thought was right,
Making me keep curfew at night,
Punishing me for coming home late
Keeping me in line… narrow and straight.
Telling me "Tomorrow's another day."
You were always right; it turned out o.k.
Looking back at life's hard times,
You were there to comfort my cries.
Very rarely missing a game
Win or lose, you hugged me the same.
Driving me where I wanted to go
Teaching me the morals I know
Dedicated, caring, honest and true
I'm proud to be your daughter…
I love you.
-Crystal Dawn Perry

My dear daughter,
You are such a delight.
Your beauty brightens this world
Morning, noon and night.
-Crystal Dawn Perry

I'm there in the morning when you wake-up
I'm there in the evening when you come home
I'm there to tell you you're wearing too much make-up
I'm there to hold you when you feel alone
I'm there to teach you wrong from right
I'm there to believe in you and give praise
I'm there in prayer for you at night.
I'll be there today, tomorrow, and always.
-Crystal Dawn Perry

I looked back in time today
And saw a little girl at play
So much like her daddy...
So much like her mother...
Yet, so much herself and like no other.
-Teresa E. Glascock

Diet

I had an extra piece of cake,
Or maybe two or three.
It wasn't long until the extra pounds
Were easy for me to see.
My clothes are tight. I'm feeling fat.
There is just one thing to do;
I'm going to start a diet
And lose a pound or two.
-Dana Roberts Clark

Discipline/Grounding
(see Trouble)

Dog
(see also Animal/Pet)

Here sits my little furry pet
Licking my face, getting me wet.
He likes to jump and play and run
But most of all he likes to love.
-Crystal Dawn Perry

Little doggie dear,
With your tongue hanging out
And funny floppy ears,
I love you more and more each day
My little doggie dear.
-Crystal Dawn Perry

Do-it-yourself/Handiwork
(see also Arts/Crafts and Talent)

Handy around the house
From the roof to the floor
It seems there's nothing left to fix
But Mom always finds more.
-Crystal Dawn Perry

Drama/School Program
(see also Talent)

Today I don't know who I am
Tomorrow I'm in love
Perhaps I'll commit a murder
Then cry to God above
Next week I may age fifty years
Or get drunk on fine wine
It's all okay as long as I
Just don't forget my line.
-Jennifer R. Shaner

I know my cue
I learned my verse
I studied my lines
Rehearsed and rehearsed
It's come my time
I'm a bundle of nerves
Will I be the show's star
Or something much worse?
-Crystal Dawn Perry

Dreams/Goals/Ambition

Working hard and dreaming dreams
Still reaching for that goal
Searching for those answers that
Live deep within your soul
Learning more about yourself
While tasting joys and tears
Carrying life's lessons in
Your heart for future years.
-Jennifer R. Shaner

Your childish dreams were fun, my son
But your dreams as a man
Will never be done
So live your life as you are-
Keep your feet firmly planted
With your head in the stars.
-Crystal Dawn Perry

Do I have what it takes?
Can I get the job done?
If anyone can do it,
I am the one.
-Crystal Dawn Perry

Reach for the stars. Go for the gold.
Be daring. Always be bold.
-Suzan L. Wiener

Easter
(See also Tradition)

There's one true reason
We celebrate this season.
In the bible, it is written:
Christ the Lord has risen!
-Crystal Dawn Perry

Early to rise
For a basket surprise
Just out of sleep
Cheep! Cheep! Cheep!
Lambs with soft fleece
White doves of peace
Peace of the lily
Eager and silly
Yellow and blue
Ducks and bunnies too
Eggs that are hidden
God's son has risen
Thank him for
These things and more
He rose above
By God's pure love.
-Crystal Dawn Perry

Exchange Student

No matter the roads you have taken
Whatever this new path will show
You're here in my heart now and always
That won't change-I want you to know.
-Jennifer R. Shaner

Excitement/Extreme Sports/Fear

I understand you're fearful and wary
But it isn't fun unless it's scary.
-Crystal Dawn Perry

Reach for the stars.
Go for the gold.
Be daring.
Always be bold.
-Suzan L. Wiener

A sense of freedom
Slicing through air
The world in a haze
I'm freed of all cares.
-Crystal Dawn Perry

My heart is racing. Danger abounds.
I'm plunging quickly toward the ground.
The excitement far exceeds the pain
So I get up and do it all over again.
-Crystal Dawn Perry

Exercise/Physique

Ridiculous! Insane!
Examine the brain
Of anyone that says,
"No Pain, No Gain"!
-Crystal Dawn Perry

Face
(see Beauty)

Family/Heritage

For the good times
And bad
Memories we've had...
I
Love
You!
  -Crystal Dawn Perry

There once was a little nut
  Swinging from a tree.
He saw he was surrounded
  By bigger nuts than he.

He learned they were relatives
Like cousins, uncles and aunts
  So he tried to run away
  But hit his head on a branch.

The big ol' nuts saw him there
  Just lying on the ground.
Soon they started jumping too
  Falling in leaps and bounds.

Now when he saw his family
  Surrounding him once again
He knew those nuts would be there for him
  No matter where or when.
  -Crystal Dawn Perry

U are special
N many ways
C how much I'll
L ways love you
E ach and every day.
-Crystal Dawn Perry

In many ways we're different
And yet we're much the same.
They have the same address as me.
We share the same last name.
There's ways we look and act alike;
At time those traits aren't cool.
We argue over stupid things
And sometimes act the fool.
Though there will be times we disagree
There's laughter, love and fun.
A family is a treasure and
I'm blessed to have this one.
-Jennifer R. Shaner

Always fun to have around
Unique in many ways
Never giving up on me
Today, tomorrow, always.
-Crystal Dawn Perry

Father
(See also Family/Heritage, Parent and Parent /Child Relationship)

Strong when you need to be,
Tough when you have to be,
Gentle when you should be;
You're everything to me.
-Crystal Dawn Perry

Daddy...
You always said I was beautiful.
You always said I was smart.
You always made me feel special.
Daddy, you'll always have my heart.
-Crystal Dawn Perry

I learned by your example,
Moral, good or bad;
I'm the person I am today
Because of you, Dad.
-Crystal Dawn Perry

Football
(See also Sports/Games and Talent)

Halfback, fullback
Running back, quarterback-
Charging up, falling back
Down the field, flying past.
-Crystal Dawn Perry

Friends/Best Friends

Different as snowflakes
Beautiful as stars
Each one an individual
Just as we are.
-Crystal Dawn Perry

We've been best friends for several years
The memories we made, I hold dear.
Some of which we can share
But I cherish the few we wouldn't dare!
-Crystal Dawn Perry

Thank you for being there,
No matter where or when
Just remember, that forever,
You'll always be my best friend.
-Suzan L. Wiener

We've laughed, we've cried
And we've laughed again
Again, and again, and again
Every day is a better day
With you as my best friend.
-Crystal Dawn Perry

From me to you,
From you to me,
Friendship is
The best gift received.
-Crystal Dawn Perry

Friends-long distance
No matter the roads you have taken
Whatever this new path will show
You're here in my heart now and always
That won't change-I want you to know.
-Jennifer R. Shaner

It's not your fault that you had to move away
But that doesn't help me today;

Today, I need you. Tomorrow, I'll miss you.
You'll be in my thoughts always.
-Crystal Dawn Perry

Too many miles separate
Without you my heart's torn
You come to me in nightly dreams
But vanish with the morn
I hope you'll soon return to me
And then my heart will mend
I need the shelter of your arms
My life, my love, my friend.
-Jennifer R. Shaner

Fun/Silliness

Really silly-
Together, you and me;
Really silly-
The best way to be!
-Crystal Dawn Perry

Today was good.
Today was fun.
Tomorrow is another one.
-Dr. Suess

Games
(see Sports/Games)

Gift

It's never too small yet it can't be large enough;
It's always just what you needed,
Even if you have an abundance.
If it is stretched, you will grow.
It can't be bought; only found.
If someone offers it to you, take it.
If you have it, you should give it away.
It is the gift that should always be returned-
The unconditional gift of love.
-Crystal Dawn Perry

God gave many
Gifts to this world
But the best gift of all
Is the gift of girls.
-Crystal Dawn Perry

To most it's just a necklace
That I wear for all to see
They'll never know its story
Or what it means to me
Reminding me of friendship
And the promise to be there
If not always in person,
At least with thoughts and prayers
They do not hear words spoken
That can give me strength to cope
Or know the touch that calms me,
Replacing fear with hope
They've never seen the smiles shared
That chased the blues away
Or known the laugh that warms me
And brightens up my day
And so I wear my necklace,
But it's like I said before
The value is the friendship,
My gift forevermore.
-Jennifer R. Shaner

From me to you,
From you to me,
Friendship is
The best gift received.
-Crystal Dawn Perry

Girls
(see also Teenager)

God gave many
Gifts to this world
But the best gift of all
Is the gift of girls.
-Crystal Dawn Perry

When God made a girl,
He gave her beautiful hair
And perfect lips.

When God made a boy
With ragged hair and big feet-
His hand must've slipped.
-Crystal Dawn Perry

The more girls change-
From dress-up and dolls
Giggles and toys
The more they stay the same-
To make-up, clothes
Giggles and boys.
-Crystal Dawn Perry

Girlfriend
(See Dating and Love)

Glasses/Contacts

I can look eye to eye
Now that I have specs
And I can see who it is
Without having to guess!
-Crystal Dawn Perry

Golf
(See also Sports/Games and Talent)

Par for the course,
He's a real swinger...
He takes a swing
But the ball lingers.
-Crystal Dawn Perry

Graduation

Actions I did
Words I said
Secrets I hid

Late nights out
Should have studied
Running about

Perseverance shown
Patience practiced
Determination grown

The Golden Rule
Highs and lows
Tired of school

Being cool
Often not
Exception to the rule

Relief, pride
Tough journey
Long ride

School is done
Future begins
At last, Graduation.
-Crystal Dawn Perry

Laughter and sweet memories
Years of work and trials
Fighting fears and dreaming dreams
Friendship, fun, and smiles

Sadness as we say good-bye
Pride within each heart
Excitement for the future
Blessed with a new start.
-Jennifer R. Shaner

It's off to higher learning
In search of a degree
Needing skills for a career
Still learning about me
Good-bye to high school days
And friends I leave behind
Ahead awaits adventure
Where dreams are mine to find.
-Jennifer R. Shaner

I want to tell the world
How proud I am of you;
How every day of your life
You've made my dreams come true.
This is your special day.
I watch, tears in my eyes,
As you get your diploma
As you say your good-byes.
Graduation is a stepping-stone
For a bright future that will last.
I know you will succeed-
You always have in the past.
-Suzan L. Wiener

Grandchild/Grandparent
(see also Family/Heritage)

Wrinkles of time looking at me
From a knowing face.
They tell a story words can't tell
Of love, experience, and grace.
-Crystal Dawn Perry

In lives distanced by many years
The differences are many
Yet hearts cannot be separated
By time, where love is plenty.
-Crystal Dawn Perry

There's no present from a grandparent
Better than the presence of mine
The best gift that can be given
Is "together time".
-Crystal Dawn Perry

You have been there from the beginning
When others could not be bothered
It is you I can depend on.
I love and respect you like no other.
-Crystal Dawn Perry

Dear Pa Paw,
You were always there in my time of need
I thank you for believing in me
And giving me the courage to succeed.

All positive things I am, I owe to you.
It was you that taught me to love myself
And to my own self be true.
Thank you.
-Crystal Dawn Perry

Growing Up
(see also Independence)

As you run in the yard, I watch from the window
Your cheeks are rosy, your hair in a bow
You're smile is as bright as morning sun
I'm grateful for this life that has just begun.
Then I'm startled when I hear a car start
Tears of joy now burn with an ache in my heart
You sit behind the wheel. You're nearly grown
How could it be that the time has flown?
You were my baby and always will be
I whisper, "I love you."
As you drive away from me.
-Crystal Dawn Perry

When I first held you, my heart filled
With more love than I had known
Yet with every inch you gain
My love for you still grows.
-Crystal Dawn Perry

Gymnastics
(see also Sports/Games and Talent)

The acrobatics
Are very dramatic
And sometimes erratic
Which is problematic
Though if systematic
It becomes automatic
Leaving all ecstatic,
Especially fanatics.
I'm not melodramatic;
I'm just charismatic
And I'm enthusiastic
For a sport that's fantastic-
I love gymnastics!
-Crystal Dawn Perry

Habit

Okay! It's true!
I admit it! I surrender!
...It's the story of my life
As a habitual offender.
-Crystal Dawn Perry

Hair

As I look at all that hair
Sometimes I wonder,
"Is anyone under there?"
-Crystal Dawn Perry

Eyes, Cheeks, Lips and Hair
These are the things for which I care
Taking the time to do them right
So I'll look hot when I go out tonight.
-Crystal Dawn Perry

Split-ended, bed-headed, in need of a trim,
Blow-dried, sun-fried, tangled in the wind,
Flat or frizzy, curly, unruly,
Smooth, shampooed, conditioned,
A hair-do never looks like new
So let's just call it a hair-did.
-Gina Marie Lauchner

Half-sibling
They call us half-sisters
But I've come to know
It takes these two halves
To make our family whole.
-Crystal Dawn Perry

One of us, I'm proud to be
He, she, we, them and me,
This awesome family
Blended perfectly.
-Crystal Dawn Perry

Halloween
Of all the goblins
That come to spook
You'll never see one
This awesomely cute!
-Crystal Dawn Perry

The sweet can be mean
The quiet can scream
Teens will be teens-
It's Halloween!
-Crystal Dawn Perry

Handicap
(See Hardship and Special Needs)

Hang-out/Special Place
Same place, same friends
Making memories and reliving old ones
Spending time with the ones we love,
Laughing over and over again.
-Crystal Dawn Perry

Memories made; moving forward
Days remembered; looking back
Togetherness, sharing, laughter,
Looking forward to coming back.
-Crystal Dawn Perry

For some it's a refuge from home
For others a haven from life
Whatever the reason for coming here
It's the people and place we like.
-Crystal Dawn Perry

Happiness
Joy, Elation, Bliss,
Delight, Pleasure, Gladness
Cheerfulness, Happiness-
You give more than all this.
-Crystal Dawn Perry

Hardship

I've been through the storm;
Now I look toward the sun.
As I reach for the rainbow,
A new day has begun.
-Crystal Dawn Perry

Mending the heart
Of someone in need
Only takes a little time
So do a kind deed.
-Crystal Dawn Perry

Days that have darkened
With heartbreak and trials
Suddenly grow brighter
With a flash of your smile.
-Crystal Dawn Perry

Hobby/Collection

Bigger is better
And better is more;
When you have a hobby
Life's less of a bore.
-Crystal Dawn Perry

Hockey
(See also Skating, Sports/Games and Talent)

Game tying, shorthanded,
Game winning, power play
I aim to score. I take a beating.
My goal in life is to play.
-Crystal Dawn Perry

Proudly wearing the jersey,
Helmet, pads, and more
Trying to keep the puck in control
And myself off the floor.
-Crystal Dawn Perry

Home

This house is our home
With memories shared
Between family and friends
And loved ones that care.
-Crystal Dawn Perry

Mid pleasures and palaces
Though we may roam,
Be it ever so humble,
There's no place like home.
-John Howard Payne

Home School
(see also School)

I'll tell you a truth
That I've come to know-
It's more fun to learn
From the comfort of home.
-Crystal Dawn Perry

Homecoming
(see also Dance)

Homecoming is finally here
As we start over a new year.
Lots of school spirit,
New friends and more fun,
A game and a dance-
The night has just begun!
-Amber D. Clark

Hug/Kiss
(see also Love)

Happiness when you give one
Understanding when you need one
Great when you receive one
-Dana Roberts Clark

Never a lip is curved with pain
That can't be kissed into smiles again.
-Bret Harte

Hunting

A steady hand, scouted land,
Patience and gun skill-
These are all essential
For your best potential
When aiming for the kill.
-Crystal Dawn Perry

Camouflage clothes,
Guns and gear;
The more money spent,
The more prey should fear
For the hunter's not happy
'Til the buck stops here.
-Crystal Dawn Perry

Illness/Injury

Ridiculous! Insane!
Examine the brain
Of anyone that says,
"No Pain, No Gain"!
-Crystal Dawn Perry

My hair is a wreck,
I'm wrinkled and smelly
But my main concern
Is this ache in my belly.
My head is pounding.
This must be the flu.
You better stay away
Or you'll get it too!
-Crystal Dawn Perry

Vaccinations, constipation, sprains
and splints and splinters
Indigestion, lozenges, Kleenex, gauze and fevers
Contusions and concussions, band-aids and bruises
Nausea and stomach aches and scrapes
and stuffed-up noses
Bacteria, infections, strep throat and stings and stitches
Laryngitis, penicillin, bumps and hives and itches
Chills and pills and viruses, vitamins, dehydration
Antiseptic, dizzy spells, bites and allergic reactions
Doctor appointments, eye drops and ointments
Cough medicine and wheezing
Chicken soup and colds and flus
Ice packs, swelling and sneezing...
-Gina Lauchner

E-I-E-I-Oh!
With a groan, groan here
And an "Ow! Ow!" there
Here a groan. There an "Ow!"
Everywhere an "Ouch! Ouch!"
Please just let me
Lie here on the couch-
E-I-E-I-Ohhhh!
-Crystal Dawn Perry

Independence

You have to let go now
I need experiences of my own
I'm not your little boy anymore
Can't you see how much I've grown?

You've led my way this far
Now I'll search for my own lesson.
I need to learn alone
To live as my own person.
-Crystal Dawn Perry

You held my hand and I thank you for that
But I'm older now; please don't hold me back.

You tug on our bond, secure and strong;
It's been "you and me" for so long.

Hold on to our memories but set me free.
I need to learn how to be just "me."
-Crystal Dawn Perry

Independence Day

Vivid sparkles
And flares in the sky
Don't compare to you,
The light of my life.
-Crystal Dawn Perry

To this great country stay true...
Salute the Red, White and Blue.
-Crystal Dawn Perry

July 4th is special.
It's a great celebration,
One that is enjoyed
Throughout our nation.
-Suzan L. Wiener

Job
(see Work)

Laziness

O bed! O bed!
Delicious bed!
That heaven upon earth
To the weary head.
-Thomas Hood

To lessen your stress,
I have the key:
Take life as it is
And live it carefree.
-Crystal Dawn Perry

Life/Everyday Moments

I've been through the storm
Now I look toward the sun
As I reach for the rainbow
A new day has begun.
-Crystal Dawn Perry

Learn to laugh.
Learn to cry.
Learn to love.
Learn to try.
Learn to be you.
Just be true.
-Natasha Fuller

You have a love for discovery;
I hope your wishes will be explored
And remember on this journey of life,
You couldn't be loved any more.
-Crystal Dawn Perry

I have new dreams
I've conquered fears
I've laugh with friends
They've dried my tears
I've blushed at jokes
I've cried at sneers...
The future and past
Of another year.
-Crystal Dawn Perry

I can't turn back the hands of time
Or change what has been done
I can't exchange the cards life dealt
Nor stop what has begun
At times I don't know what to say
I'm scared to show my heart
I'm sometimes awkward and confused
On how to play my part
But nothing that I say or do
Can give me the control
Of what was never in my hands
But battles with my soul.
-Jennifer R. Shaner

Love
(see also Dating)

I never knew three little words
Could ever mean so much
Until I looked into your eyes
And felt your sweet soft touch.
"I love you."
-Dana Roberts Clark

Like a rainbow out of reach
It is your love I seek.
-Crystal Dawn Perry

I often wish for a fine, gallant knight
On a beautiful white horse
But you with your tattered tennis shoes
And beaten up bicycle are much finer.
I'd like to feel the finest silk about my skin
But I'm much more comfortable in a pair of jeans
And your arms about my waist.
I'd like to be given great riches
Like diamonds, emerald, or pearls
But you give me hope, love and happiness-
The greatest riches of all.
-Jill T. Ardary

You look like an angel from above...
In your presence I blush.
It feels more than a crush.
Oh, no! I think I'm in love!
-Crystal Dawn Perry

When I first held you, my heart filled
With more love than I had known
Yet with every day that passes
My love for you still grows.
-Crystal Dawn Perry

Take me in your arms
Near your pounding heart
Tell me it beats for me
And we'll never be apart.
-Crystal Dawn Perry

You have been there from the beginning
When others could not be bothered
It is you I can depend on.
I love and respect you like no other.
-Crystal Dawn Perry

It's never too small yet it can't be large enough;
It's always just what you needed,
Even if you have an abundance.
If it is stretched, you will grow.
It can't be bought; only found.
If someone offers it to you, take it.
If you have it, you should give it away.
It is the gift that should always be returned-
The unconditional gift of love.
-Crystal Dawn Perry

He came to me at midnight
With magic in his eyes.
His strong arms were around me.
We never thought of good-byes.
He seemed so endearing
As his tender lips kissed mine.
I only thought of that moment
Lasting 'til the end of time.
Now I know what real love is.
It's filled with pure bliss.
That is why I thank you
For all my happiness.
-Suzan L. Wiener

I really do love you.
You're the highlight of my day.
You bring in the brightness
That always lights my way.
-Suzan L. Wiener

Destiny brought you into my life.
I have never felt a love so right.
You are the half that makes me whole.
You are the one who fills my soul.
-Dana Roberts Clark

Make-up

Eyes, Cheeks, Lips and Hair
These are the things for which I care
Taking the time to do them right
So I'll look hot when I go out tonight.
-Crystal Dawn Perry

Memories

Growing up, we shared it all
Now, we're growing our own ways.
No matter where life takes me to,
In my heart, our memories stay.
-Crystal Dawn Perry

Same place, same friends
Making memories and reliving old ones
Spending time with the ones we love,
Laughing over and over again.
-Crystal Dawn Perry

We've been best friends for several years
The memories we made, I hold dear.
Some of which we can share
But I cherish the few we wouldn't dare!
-Crystal Dawn Perry

Memory of a Loved One
(see also Memories)

Keep my picture in a frame
Keep my memory in mind
Keep my love in your heart
Keep my kiss in your dreams.
Keep your dreams alive
And always know...
Our love will be for keeps.
-Crystal Dawn Perry

It's mystery and misery
Why the good die young.
How could life's best end
When the best had just begun?
-Crystal Dawn Perry

Remember me when I am gone away,
Gone away into the silent land;
When you can no more hold me by the hand,
Nor I half turn to go, yet turning to stay;
Remember me when no more, day by day.
-Christina Rossetti

Military

To this great country stay true...
Salute the Red, White and Blue.
-Crystal Dawn Perry

I was taught responsibility
And to stand for what's right
I will protect your safety
And defend your rights

I don't need a hero's welcome
A simple "Thank you" is fine
With an understanding of why
Our flag is allowed to fly

It's because of women and men
Who cared enough to join the service
So when you see a flag wave proudly
Please remember this-

There's a price to be paid
You're freedom is not free
America was bought
By soldiers like me.
-Crystal Dawn Perry

Remember when you held his hand,
And made him groan when asked to stand
Through pledges as we stood and watched
The flag unfurled and staunchly marched?

Remember when he had those fights
And you defended all his rights
And you taught him to protect what's his
And see the world for what it is?

Today your boy is now a man
Who's living all your life commands
Where once you sheltered as he grew
He leaves today, to protect you.
-R. Dee Waltz-Daniels

Money
(see Work)

Mother
(see also Family/Heritage, Parent and Parent/Child Relationship)

Being a mother means...
Being blessed, being tired, prayers sent above
Dreams for your child, hopes thought of,
Emotions recognized, unconditional love,
Never-ending laundry and never-ending love.
-Crystal Dawn Perry

From the beginning
Together 'til the end
The keeper of my heart,
My mother, my friend.
-Crystal Dawn Perry

My mother would move land and sea
If I said they were in my way.

She often traded her dreams for mine
With no more than a hug for pay.

Thinking of all she's done for me
I can hear my heart say,

If I had asked her for the moon
I would be holding the world today.
-Crystal Dawn Perry

Movies/Television

A great way
To hang with friends
Watching the screen
For hours on end
So grab a snack
It's time for the show
The plot will grow
As the story unfolds.
-Crystal Dawn Perry

Sadness, laughter
Trouble, screams
The bigger the better
On the movie screen.
-Crystal Dawn Perry

Multiples
(see also Sibling)

You are so much more
Than half of one
And yet you're each
Second to none!
-Crystal Dawn Perry

Our matching outfits were a little too cute
And our bottles often got switched.
I get tired of playing "who is who?"
But enjoy the confusing tricks.
It often feels like a losing battle
In this challenge of being a twin
But because I have you as a match
Life has dealt me a win.
-Crystal Dawn Perry

If every time I saw you
I asked where someone else was at
And I made you feel like only half,
What would you think of that?
-Crystal Dawn Perry

Music

Don't say a word.
Just close your eyes.
Listen to the music
And let your heart guide.
-Crystal Dawn Perry

Music is to be...
Heard with the heart
Seen by the sound
Felt with the soul;
Harmony surrounds.
-Crystal Dawn Perry

New Year

My heart fills with wishes
And dreams to come true
Of spending this evening
And the New Year with you.
-Crystal Dawn Perry

I have new dreams
I've conquered fears
I've laughed with friends
They've dried my tears
I've blushed at jokes
I've cried at sneers...
The future and past
Of another year.
-Crystal Dawn Perry

A new year
For love
A new year
For heartache
A new year
To give
A new year
To take
A new year
To forget
A new year
To forgive
A new year
To dream
A new year
To live.
-Crystal Dawn Perry

Parade

Standing tall, instrument in hand,
Making sure to reach the mark
Staying in step, sounding out,
Inspiring crowds as we march.
-Crystal Dawn Perry

Parent
(See also Family/Heritage, Father, Mother and Parent/Child Relationship)

Let me introduce you
To my torments.
Oops! Freudian slip-
I meant to say, "to my parents."
-Crystal Dawn Perry

Go get it for me. Sit in time-out.
Don't touch that. You must share.
Sit up straight. Make your bed.
Brush your teeth. Comb your hair.
Turn down the music. Turn off the TV.
Clean up your room. Drive with more care.
No matter what I wanted to do, you were there...
Thank you.
-Crystal Dawn Perry

I'm there in the morning when you wake-up
I'm there in the evening when you come home
I'm there to tell you you're wearing too much make-up
I'm there to hold you when you feel alone
I'm there to teach you wrong and right
I'm there to believe in you and give praise
I'm there in prayer for you at night.
I'll be there today, tomorrow, and always.
-Crystal Dawn Perry

Parent/Child Relationship
(See also Family/Heritage, Father, Mother and Parent)

When you broke your promise
You broke my heart too.
I grew up missing something-
That something was you.
-Crystal Dawn Perry

Where is my child that would cry in the night
And wouldn't stop 'til I held him tight?
At times he would say, "Mommy, I need you."
Maybe I didn't say it but I needed him too.
Where is my child that gave me sweet hugs?
My heartstrings long to feel that tug.
I loved him then as I love him now;
I want to reach him but I don't know how.
If you should pass him along life's path,
Tell him his mother needs him back.
-Crystal Dawn Perry

There were times when I thought you didn't care
But now I can see you were always there.
Some of your actions I didn't understand.
I admit I resented your upper hand.
You were doing what you thought was right,
Making me keep curfew at night,
Punishing me for coming home late
Keeping me in line... narrow and straight.
Telling me "Tomorrow's another day."
You were always right; it turned out o.k.
Looking back at life's hard times,
You were there to comfort my cries.
Very rarely missing a game
Win or lose, you hugged me the same.
Driving me where I wanted to go
Teaching me the morals that I know
Dedicated, caring, honest and true
I'm proud to be your daughter...
I love you.
-Crystal Dawn Perry

The rules for parents are but three...
love, limit, and let them be.
-Elaine M. Ward

You have been there from the beginning
When others could not be bothered
It is you I can depend on.
I love and respect you like no other.
-Crystal Dawn Perry

When I ask if I can help you
I'm not saying that you can't do it
It's just one way of showing that I care.

If I tell you to be careful
When you're not within my sight
More than worry, it's wishing I were there.

True, we may not share the same beliefs
Or dreams I have for you
We battle over wants and choices made.

But understand it's hard sometimes
As I watch you make your way
My love remains as childhood starts to fade.
-Jennifer R. Shaner

Party

Hot Girls, Hot Guys,
And all of my best friends
If this party is a dream
I hope the night never ends.
-Crystal Dawn Perry

Invitation
Decorations
Location
Temptation...
Celebration!
-Crystal Dawn Perry

Passover

Passed over by the Lord
To freedom's way
Passover...
That exalted day.
-Crystal Dawn Perry

Prom
(see also Dance and Dating)

Excited to be going
Trying to stay calm
I can't believe
The time has come-
I'm going to the prom!
-Crystal Dawn Perry

Beautiful dress, hair just right,
Glitter, fantasy, a magical night.

Prom night makes a young girl shine
And feel like floating on cloud nine!
-Laura Taylor Mark

Perfect
Romance...
Our
Memories
-Crystal Dawn Perry

Rock-Climbing
(see also Excitement/Extreme Sports/Fear)

Slow and steady, there's no need to race
Just take your time being sure to brace
If you should fall it would be a disgrace;
Getting stuck between a rock and hard place.
-Crystal Dawn Perry

Running
(see also Sports/Games and Talent)

A sense of freedom
Slicing through air
The world in a haze
Freed of all cares.
-Crystal Dawn Perry

Run like the wind
Until the road ends
From start to finish
We'll be fast friends.
-Crystal Dawn Perry

School

Laughing, flirting
Halfway learning
Hanging with my friends

Attending classes
Time slowly passes
Until the school day ends.
-Crystal Dawn Perry

Working hard to make the grade
Reports and tests galore
Books piled high upon the desk
Papers on the floor
Candy wrappers next to me
Drink stains on my book
Don't know how much time has passed
Just too tired to look.
-Jennifer R. Shaner

School begins.
The day ends.
Get up and do it
All over again.
-Crystal Dawn Perry

Scrapbooking
(see also Arts/Crafts, Hobby/Collection, Memories and Talent)

Memories of family, friendship, joy and tears
Will live forever in my heart and mind.
Here's my way of sharing them in the coming years
With those I love and new friends I may find.
-Jennifer R. Shaner

Just look at this clutter, look at this mess!
Oh, where did I put that green paper dress?
Now digging through piles of rainbow debris
Oh, no! Not this paper! It's not acid free!

Where are those scissors? I know I just had 'em!
Excuse me, but those are MY photos, madam.
Stickers! My stickers! Oh, where can they be?
I grumble but I do LOVE to scrapbook, you see.
-T.R. Cardinet

Shopping

Grab the keys
There's no time to spare
The mall is open
I've got to get there!
-Crystal Dawn Perry

Sibling
(see also Brother, Family/Heritage, Sister)

Growing up, we shared it all
Now, we're growing our own ways.
No matter where life takes me to,
In my heart, our memories stay.
-Crystal Dawn Perry

Different as snowflakes
Beautiful as stars
Each one an individual
Just as we are.
-Crystal Dawn Perry

Mother always taught me,
"Be kind to others."
But I'm sure she didn't mean
To my sister and brother.
-Crystal Dawn Perry

Brother to Sister,
Sister to Brother,
I will love and defend you
Like no other.
-Crystal Dawn Perry

Through the days of torture and days of laughter
It was the senseless things that often mattered
But as we change, we'll come to know
As the silliness passes to long ago
Fights will fade and love grows strong
It's each other that mattered, all along.
-Crystal Dawn Perry

Sister
(see also Family/Heritage and Sibling)

Little sister is a nuisance.
Little sister is a pain.
Little sister seems to get pleasure
Out of driving me insane.

Little sister makes me angry.
Little sister makes me mad.
Little sister makes me sometimes wish
A little sister I never had.

But, if anyone wants to harm her
They first have to come through me,
For although little sister's annoying
She's still little sister to me.
-Linda Hayes

She has slugged me
She has hugged me
She has hated me
She has loved me
Seen my good side
Seen my bad
Told our Mom
Sided with Dad
She broke my heart
She made me laugh
My sister always;
My friend at last.
-Crystal Dawn Perry

Giggles, secrets,
Sometimes tears,
Sister and Friends
Throughout the years.
-Unknown

Skateboarding
(See also Excitement/Extreme Sports/Fear)

Hangin' ten.
Hangin' tough.
Bigger is better.
Better is rough.
-Crystal Dawn Perry

Skating
(See also Excitement/Extreme Sports/Fear)

If I could freeze time
I would spend it on ice
Freezing every moment
Spent gliding through life.
-Crystal Dawn Perry

One day you'll see me
On E.S.P.N.
Then you can say,
"I knew him when..."
-Crystal Dawn Perry

Graceful gliding strokes
With beauty and artistry
Such overwhelming joy
As skating sets you free.
-Brenda Darlene Kijowski

Skiing
(See also Skating)

It looks so easy
On the sport shows-
Just strap on the skis,
Push off, and g-ohhhh!
-Crystal Dawn Perry

Sleepover

Snacks and gossip,
Staying awake,
Telling stories,
Laughing 'til we ache.
-Crystal Dawn Perry

Sleep now, Oh, sleep now,
Oh, you unquiet heart!
A voice crying "Sleep now"
Is heard in my heart.
-James Joyce

Snow

Glitter cascades to the ground,
Scattering the joy it makes.
Drifting carelessly among the sound
Of laughter swirling between the flakes.
-Crystal Dawn Perry

Throw, build, run, and play
Laugh, chill...SNOW DAY!
-Crystal Dawn Perry

Soccer
(see also Sports/Games and Talent)

Down the field,
You're the defender.
Kick it back,
Past the goal-tender.
Whether attacking
Or you're the blocker,
It takes the whole team
For a great game of soccer.
-Crystal Dawn Perry

Softball
(see also Sports/Games and Talent)

The players on the field yell,
"Swing! Batter! Batter!"
The fans in the bleachers
Start to swelter
The air smells
Of hotdogs and dirt
The bat swings
And the crowd goes berserk!
-Crystal Dawn Perry

Son
(see also Boys, Family/Heritage and Teenager)

When you were just a little boy,
We used to wonder what you would do when you grew up...
Would you be a doctor? A cowboy? An engineer?
And when you became a teenager,
We worried about you, often shedding tears.
Now, when I look at you
I see all that you are and all that you will be
And I realize the concern we've had in past years
Was nothing more than unproven fears.
-Crystal Dawn Perry

You have to let go now
I need experiences of my own
I'm not your little boy anymore
Can't you see how much I've grown?

You've led my way this far
Now I'll search for my own lesson.
I need to learn alone
To live as my own person.
-Crystal Dawn Perry

Your childish dreams were fun, my son
But your dreams as a man
Will never be done.
So live your life as you are
Keep your feet firmly planted
With your head in the stars.
-Crystal Dawn Perry

I hope the warmth given by you
Is reflected back by my love too
Brightening my life from day one
My heart shines for you, my "son."
-Crystal Dawn Perry

Special Needs
(see also Hardship)

They said you couldn't.
You showed them you could.
They said you wouldn't.
You knew you would.

With special love
And extra needs
Through your strength and courage
I've learned to believe.

Thank you for being special.
-Crystal Dawn Perry

Sports/Games
(see also Excitement/Extreme Sports/Fear, Talent and Specific Sports)

One day you'll see me
On E.S.P.N.
Then you can say,
"I knew him when…"
-Crystal Dawn Perry

The stands are scattered
With members of the band
Friends meeting friends
And loyal fans

There for support
For an unpleasant end
Or singing the praises
Of their team in a win.
-Crystal Dawn Perry

Don't be deceived
By the make-up and hair.
These girls are as tough
As any male player.
-Crystal Dawn Perry

Passion or obsession,
Call it what you will.
I've gotta do
What I've gotta do-
I've got to WIN!
-Crystal Dawn Perry

Spring Break
Bikinis and flip-flops,
That's all I should take.
What more could I need
On the beach at Spring Break?
-Crystal Dawn Perry

A little madness in the Spring
Is wholesome even for the King.
-Emily Dickinson

St. Patrick's Day

Oh, I wish, I wish
On a four-leaf clover
To have a kiss
From an Irish lover.
-Crystal Dawn Perry

May your neighbors respect you,
Trouble neglect you
The angels protect you,
And heaven accept you.
-Irish blessing

May your thoughts be as glad as the Shamrocks,
May your heart be as light as a song
May each day bring you bright, happy hours,
That stay with you all the year long.
-Irish Blessing

Step-Parent/Step-Sibling

When you came into my life
I admit I was cautious.
Who was this stranger
Trying to be one of us?

"Step-parent" was always
What other kids had.
The thought made me angry,
Uncertain and mad.

Now, over time
It has become clear.
We are all family-
That's a thought I hold dear.
-Crystal Dawn Perry

One of us, I'm proud to be
He, she, we, them and me,
This awesome family
Blended perfectly.
-Crystal Dawn Perry

When we were alone,
You stepped in.
When we were down,
You stepped up.

You know when to take charge
Or when to step down.
You are a step above the rest...
The best step-parent around.
-Crystal Dawn Perry

Style
Looking good
From head to toe
Need fashion tips?
Just let me know!
-Crystal Dawn Perry

Might I suggest
Some are a mess
From a lot of stress
To dress to impress
And be the best dressed
But I'm not depressed
For I have been blessed
With the style I possess
Though I'm a little obsessed
With this never-ending quest
To stand out from the rest
And look my best.
-Crystal Dawn Perry

Summer

The lazy days of summer-
The grass continues to grow
No chance for me to be lazy
Once again, I have to mow.
-Crystal Dawn Perry

Camping under starry skies
Or splashing in the pool
Time to laugh and hang with friends
But best of all-no school!
-Jennifer R. Shaner

Summer means...
Butterflies, flowers,
Green grass and sun,
Open windows, laughter,
No school and fun.
-Crystal Dawn Perry

Sunbathing

The best way I can think of
To spend a summer day
Is to look hot and be cool
While soaking up the rays.
-Crystal Dawn Perry

Sunglasses

My personality shines
Like the summer's glow,
So I wear these sunglasses
Wherever I go.
-Crystal Dawn Perry

Surfing
(see also Excitement/Extreme Sports/Fear)

Hangin' ten.
Hangin' tough.
Bigger is better.
Better is rough.
-Crystal Dawn Perry

Swimming/Water Sports

Eating, sleeping
And going to school-
Just passing time
'Til I get to the pool.
-Crystal Dawn Perry

Errors, like straws,
Upon the surface flow;
He who would search for pearls,
Must dive below.
-John Dryden

Swimming through time
To view life from the start
In search of treasures
That have flooded my heart.
-Crystal Dawn Perry

Camping under starry skies
Or splashing in the pool
Time to laugh and hang with friends
But best of all-no school!
-Jennifer R. Shaner

Ocean, river,
Lake or pool,
Fun or sport,
It's all cool.
-Crystal Dawn Perry

Talent
A master of the craft,
Second to none
Always impressing
With a job well done.
-Crystal Dawn Perry

"I don't know
How you do what you do?!"...
It just comes naturally
When I do it for you.
-Crystal Dawn Perry

Do I have what it takes?
Can I get the job done?
If anyone can do it,
I am the one.
-Crystal Dawn Perry

Teenager
(See also Boys, Character/Personality, Girls, Growing Up, Independence and Life/Everyday Moments)

Years ago in your childish dreams,
You were ready to take on the world.
Now in your dreams, you leave your youth.
I hope the world is ready for you.
-Crystal Dawn Perry

I stand before the mirror
And look for what they see
Why is it that so many
Have such different views of me?

Some tell me I'm pretty
Some say I have big feet
There are those who say I'm immature
But many think I'm neat

Teachers brag I'm very smart
Friends joke that I'm crazy
So I study my reflection
But all I see is me.
-Jennifer R. Shaner

Working hard and dreaming dreams
Still reaching for that goal
Searching for those answers that
Live deep within your soul
Learning more about yourself
While tasting joys and tears
Carrying life's lessons
In your heart for future years.
-Jennifer R. Shaner

A foot in two words, caught in between,
Sometimes it's so hard to be a teen-
Old enough to lend a helping hand
Too young to make "them" understand.
-T.R. Cardinet

Telephone

You and I make a connection
It's been clear from the start
I vowed to keep my distance
But then you roamed into my heart

I know how to turn you on
I know what buttons to push
Shh! I think I hear my mom
Hold on a minute...Hush...

She says, "Don't spend another minute..."
But I need you every day
If she catches us together again
There will be a high price to pay

I don't care though-
It's you that keeps me grounded
What she says is just chatter to me
The charges are unfounded

I long to take you in my hands
Pulling you close to my face
Including nights and weekends,
Any time, any place

When your face lights up
My heart plays a tune
Our shared time together
Is long overdue

You've heard it said over and over,
"Communication is the key"
Talking to you is my calling
It couldn't be easier for me

The vibration I get from you
Opens my heart to receive
And I live for the moment
When you'll give me a ring

As long as I have you,
I will never be alone,
You're my connection to life...
My priceless cell phone.
-Crystal Dawn Perry

Tennis/Racquetball
(see also Sports/Games and Talent)

A match of speed, muscle and skill
Not a game for the weak
But the strong of will.
-Crystal Dawn Perry

Thanksgiving
(see also Tradition)

Thanksgiving Day:
A time to reflect.
I can't feel thankful
But I wish for the best.

Heartache, pain,
Broken friendships and more
What do I have
To be thankful for?

I am thankful that
One day this will pass
Then these thankless years
Will be history at last.
-Crystal Dawn Perry

A time for thanks
A time to pray
For our many blessings
Thanksgiving Day.
-Crystal Dawn Perry

Thank you Lord
For all you give
A grateful heart
A passion to live
The sun and the stars
The land and the sea
Given with love
Given to me.
-Crystal Dawn Perry

Tradition

Memories made; moving forward
Days remembered; looking back
Togetherness, sharing, laughter,
Looking forward to coming back.
-Crystal Dawn Perry

Same place, same friends
Making memories and reliving old ones
Spending time with the ones we love,
Laughing over and over again.
-Crystal Dawn Perry

Travel

For many a pleasant mile -
Link-armed and dumb they travel,
They sing not, but they smile.
-Robert Louis Stevenson

Trouble

These walls have me surrounded.
Mom said my story is unfounded
Wasn't as good as I thought it sounded
So here I sit in my room, grounded.
-Crystal Dawn Perry

Momma always said
"Here comes trouble."
But she couldn't have known
I would cause it double!
-Crystal Dawn Perry

Go get it for me. Sit in time-out.
Don't touch that. You must share.
Sit up straight. Make your bed.
Brush your teeth. Comb your hair.
Turn down the music. Turn off the TV.
Clean up your room. Drive with more care.
No matter what I wanted to do, you were there...
Thank you.
-Crystal Dawn Perry

Okay! It's true!
I admit it! I surrender!
...It's the story of my life
As a habitual offender.
-Crystal Dawn Perry

Uncle
(see Family/Heritage)

Vacation

Memories made; moving forward
Days remembered; looking back
Togetherness, sharing, laughter,
Looking forward to coming back.
-Crystal Dawn Perry

Lazy days, fun-filled nights
Dining, shopping, seeing sights
Vacation is the time to do
Whatever brings great joy to you!
-Laura Taylor Mark

Valentine's Day
(see also Love)

I sensed he was upon me
So from love I hid.

I ran from stupid cupid
But my heart braked and I slid.

I tried to dodge his glances
For to pierce my heart he bid.

He needn't use an arrow,
With my true love's eyes he did.
-Crystal Dawn Perry

I need you so.
I need you, I do.
You are my Valentine
...how much I want you.
-Suzan L. Wiener

You excite my heart
With the love you display.
You warm my heart
With the things you say.
You hold my heart
Forever and always.
Please be mine
On Valentine's Day.
-Crystal Dawn Perry

Volleyball
(see also Sports/Games and Talent)

Serve, set, bump, spike
Control the ball.
Rotate, block, side-out
Referee's call.
Team work, do your part...
Win above all.
-Crystal Dawn Perry

Volunteer Work

Mending the heart
Of someone in need
Only takes a little time
So do a kind deed.
-Crystal Dawn Perry

Do you have what it takes?
Can you get the job done?
If anyone can do it,
I am the one.
-Crystal Dawn Perry

With a brilliant mind
And your acts so kind
Thoughtful and smart...
Love grows in your heart.
-Crystal Dawn Perry

Work
(see also Talent)

Work, work, work-
It's such a bore.
At times, life feels like
One big chore.
-Crystal Dawn Perry

"I need a job", I heard you say
"To pay my bills and my own way."
So now with money, here you are-
Dressed to a tee and with your own car.
-Margo Dill

Getting paid to learn new skills.
Too bad so much goes for bills.
Still this work that I must do
Gets me cash for fun times too.
-Jennifer R. Shaner

Wrestling
(see also Sports/Games and Talent)

Knees skinned,
Out of wind;
It's worth it all
To win with a pin.
-Crystal Dawn Perry

Yard Work
(see Chores)

Poems

The Write TEEN Words

Poems

Poems

I didn't say that I didn't say it.
I said that I didn't say that I said it.
I want to make that very clear.
-George Romney

Quotes

Adoption/Foster Child
(see also Home and Step-parent/Step-sibling)

Where I was born and
where and how I have lived is unimportant.
It is what I have done with where I have been
that should be of interest.
-Georgia O'Keefe

Becoming a mother makes you the mother of all children.
From now on each wounded, abandoned frightened child
is yours. You live in the suffering mothers of every race and
creed and weep with them.
You long to comfort all who are desolate.
-Charlotte Gray

Blessed are they who heal us of self-despisings.
Of all services which can be done to man,
I know of none more precious.
-William Hale White

I am I plus my circumstances.
-Jose Ortega y Gasset

Amusement Park
(see also Excitement/Extreme Sports/Fear)

Love doesn't make the world go 'round.
Love is what makes the ride worthwhile.
-Franklin P. Jones

If I had my life to live over, I would start barefoot
earlier in the summer and stay that way later in the fall.
I would go to more dances.
I would ride more merry-go-rounds.
-Nadine Stair

I look just like the girl next door...
if you happen to live next door to an amusement park.
-Dolly Parton

The real character of a man is found out by his amusements.
-Joshua Reynolds

Anguish/Despondency

Youth is a mortal wound.
-Katherine Paterson

We are all born mad. Some remain so.
-Samuel Beckett

People say that you're going the wrong way,
when it's simply a way of your own.
-Angelina Jolie

Some day they will know what I mean.
-Tom Thomson

Mad, bad and dangerous to know.
-Lady Caroline Lamb

To be alone is to be different. To be different is to be alone.
-Suzanne Gordon

To be nobody but yourself –
in a world which is doing its best,
night and day, to make you everybody else-
means to fight the hardest battle which any human being
can fight, and never stop fighting.
-e.e. cummings

As we drive along this road of life,
occasionally a gal will find herself a little lost;
and when that happens, I guess she has to
let go of the coulda, shoulda, woulda,
buckle up and just keep going.
-Sarah Jessica Parker

Blessed are they who heal us of self-despisings.
Of all services which can be done to man,
I know of none more precious.
-William Hale White

Adolescence is like cactus.
-Anais Nin

Animal/Pet
(see also Cat and Dog)

Our perfect companions never have fewer than four feet.
-Colette

Animals are such agreeable friends...
They ask no questions; they pass no criticisms.
-George Eliot

There is no better trade-off in this world
than a stray animal which exchanges love for a bowl of food.
-Crystal Dawn Perry

All animals are equal
but some animals are more equal than others.
-George Orwell

Of all the animals, the boy is the most unmanageable.
-Plato

"Just living is not enough," said the butterfly.
"One must have sunshine, freedom, and a little flower."
-Hans Christian Andersen

Horses make a landscape look beautiful.
-Loretta Gage

The snake stood up for evil in the garden.
-Robert Frost

All animals except man
know that the ultimate point of life is to enjoy it.
-Samuel Butler

Arts/Crafts
(see also Talent)

Painting is just another way of keeping a diary.
-Pablo Picasso

For me, painting is a way to forget life.
It is a cry in the night, a strangled laugh.
-Georges Rouault

May no gift be too small to give, nor too simple to receive,
which is wrapped in thoughtfulness and tied with love.
-L.O. Baird

I found I could say things with color and shapes
that I couldn't say any other way-
things I had no words for.
-Georgia O'Keefe

The hand can never execute anything
higher than the heart can inspire.
-Ralph Waldo Emerson

Art is the only way to run away without leaving home.
-Twyla Tharp

Attitude/Ego

I may have faults but being wrong ain't one of them.
-Jimmy Hoffa

We are all worms, but I do believe that I am a glow-worm.
-Winston Churchill

The greatest discovery of any generation is that human
beings can alter their lives by altering their attitudes.
-Albert Schweitzer

Mad, bad and dangerous to know.
-Lady Caroline Lamb

I'm one of those people you hate because of genetics.
It's the truth.
-Brad Pitt

There must be more to life than having everything!
-Maurice Sendak

I am as bad as the worst,
but Thank God, I am as good as the best.
-Walt Whitman

My theory is that if you look confident
you can pull off anything–
even if you have no clue what you're doing.
-Jessica Alba

I find myself fascinating.
-Richard Dreyfess

Tell me I'm clever, tell me I'm kind, tell me I'm talented,
tell me I'm cute, tell me I'm sensitive, graceful and wise,
tell me I'm perfect- but tell me the truth.
-Shel Silverstein

When you're as great as I am, it's hard to be humble.
-Muhammad Ali

Aunt
(see Family/Heritage)

Babysitting

A baby is always more trouble than you thought
-and more wonderful.
-Charles Osgood

Changing a diaper is a lot like getting a present
from your grandmother -you're not sure what you've got
but you're pretty sure you're not going to like it.
-Jeff Foxworthy

Few things help an individual more
than to place responsibility upon him,
and to let him know that you trust him.
-Booker T. Washington

The fundamental job of a toddler is to rule the universe.
-Lawrence Kutner

I figure if the kids are alive at the end of the day,
I've done my job.
-Rosanne Barr

Band/Musical Instruments
(see also Music and Talent)

We few. We happy few. We band of brothers.
-William Shakespeare

Hats off! Along the street there comes a blare of bugles,
a ruffle of drums, a flash of color beneath the sky;
Hats off! The flag is passing by.
-Henry Holcomb Bennett

For better or worse, you must play
your own little instrument in the orchestra of life.
-Dale Carnegie

An instrument is nothing until it is lifted.
-Kathryn Hulme

To give yourself the best possible chance of playing to your potential, you must prepare for every eventuality.
That means practice.
-Steve Ballesteros

To appreciate the skill of baton twirling, you must take the baton confidently in your hand, stand proud and make sure everyone is looking at you. Now, twist it around your fingers, throw it in the air, and run!
-Crystal Dawn Perry

Music is your own experience-
your thoughts, your wisdom.
If you don't live it, it won't come out of your horn.
-Charlie Parker

I shut my eyes in order to see.
-Paul Gauguin

Baton technique is to a conductor
what fingers are to a pianist.
-Igor Markevitch

Life is like a piano-
what you get out of it depends on how you play it.
-Tom Lehrer

The fibers of all things have their tensions
and are strained like the string of an instrument.
-Henry David Thoreau

The flute is not an instrument that has a good moral effect;
it is too exciting.
-Aristotle

For a crowd is not company;
and faces are but a gallery of pictures; And talk but a
tinkling cymbal where there is no love.
-Francis Bacon

There are two instruments that are worse than a clarinet-
two clarinets.
-Ambrose Bierce

Baseball
(see also Sports/Games and Talent)

The other sports are just sports. Baseball is a love.
-Bryant Gumbel

Baseball, it is said, is only a game. True.
And the Grand Canyon is only a hole in Arizona.
-George F. Will

Don't forget to swing hard, in case you hit the ball.
-Woodie Held

I don't want to play golf.
When I hit a ball, I want someone else to go chase it.
-Rogers Hornsby

Basketball
(See also Sports/Games and Talent)

Big shots are only little shots who keep shooting.
-Christopher Morley

You miss 100% of the shots you don't take.
-Wayne Gretzky

Any American boy can be a basketball star
if he grows up, up, up.
-Bill Vaughn

What you are as a person is far more important
than what you are as a basketball player.
-John Wooden

Beach
(See also Swimming/Water Sports and Travel)

Forget not that the earth delights to feel your bare feet
and the winds long to play with your hair.
-Kahlil Gibran

You cannot discover new oceans
unless you have the courage to lose sight of the shore.
-Italian proverb

Some things have been difficult to tame: the oceans, fools,
and women. We may soon be able to tame the oceans;
fools and women will take a little longer.
-Spiro T. Agnew

I'm an ocean... I'm really deep.
If you search deep enough you can find
rare exotic treasures.
-Christina Aguilera

One cannot collect all the beautiful shells on the beach.
One can collect only a few,
and they are more beautiful if they are few.
-Anne Morrow Lindbergh

The beach was crowded; people tossed like ripe corn,
buttering themselves as they went.
-Anne Sexton

Don't make waves.
-Belgian proverb

Beauty

Do you love me because I'm beautiful,
or am I beautiful because you love me?
-Oscar Hammerstein, II

Thin people are beautiful but fat people are adorable.
-Jackie Gleason

When I lay my head on the pillow at night,
I can say I was a decent person today;
that's when I feel beautiful.
-Drew Barrymore

Nature makes boys and girls lovely to look upon
so they can be tolerated until they acquire some sense.
-William Lyon Phelps

Beauty is not caused. It is.
-Emily Dickinson

Bedroom

Infinite riches in a little room.
-Christopher Marlowe

Children are a house's enemy. They don't mean to be –
they just can't help it. It's their enthusiasm, their energy,
their naturally destructive tendencies.
-Delia Ephron

You must have a room,
for a certain hour or so a day…
a place where you can simply experience and bring forth
what you are and what you might be.
-Joseph Campbell

Have a place for everything
and keep the things somewhere else.
That is not advice, it is merely custom.
-Mark Twain

My mother was an authority on pigsties:
"This is the worst-looking pigsty
I have ever seen in my life,
and I want it cleaned up right now!"
-Bill Cosby

Birthday
(see also Gift and Party)

Your birthday is a special time
to celebrate the gift of you to the world.
-Unknown

Sooner or later we all discover that the important moments
in life are not the advertised ones, not the birthdays,
the graduations, the weddings,
not the great goals achieved.
The real milestones are less prepossessing.
They come to the door of memory.
-Susan B. Anthony

Growing older sucks...
It just means there's been more time
for crap to happen to you.
-Paula Roche

We are all born mad. Some remain so.
-Samuel Beckett

I was born not knowing
and have had only a little time to change
that here and there.
-Richard Feynman

There was a star danced, and under that was I born.
-William Shakespeare

Books

By words, the mind is winged.
-Aristophanes

The beauty of the written word is that
it can be held close to the heart
and read over and over again.
-Florence Littauer

I find television very educating.
Every time somebody turns on the set,
I go into the other room and read a book.
-Groucho Marx

Bowling

Having a family
is like having a bowling alley installed in your brain.
-Martin Mull

The bowling alley is the poor man's country club.
-Sanford Hansell

We are all in the gutter,
but some of us are looking at the stars.
-Oscar Wilde

Wait long; strike fast.
-Chinese proverb

Boxing/Fighting
(see also Sports/Games and Talent)

Float like a butterfly, sting like a bee.
-Muhammad Ali

I might get knocked out, but I'm going to fail swinging.
-Will Smith

To me, boxing is like a ballet, except there's no music,
no choreography, and the dancers hit each other.
-Jack Handey

Fall seven times, stand up eight.
-Japanese Proverb

Boyfriend
(see Dating and Love)

Boys
(see also Teenager)

Boys are beyond the range of anybody's full understanding,
At least when they are between the ages of
18 months and 90 years.
-James Thurber

Of all the animals, the boy is the most unmanageable.
-Plato

Boys will be boys. And even that wouldn't matter
if only we could prevent girls from being girls.
-Anthony Hope Hawkins

A boy becomes an adult three years before his parents
think he does, and about two years after he thinks he does.
-Lewis B. Hershey

Teenage boys, goaded by their surging hormones
run in packs like the primal horde.
-Camille Paglia

Girls we love for what they are;
young men for what they promise to be.
-Johann Wolfgang Von Goethe

Boys will be boys.
-American proverb

When I grow up I want to be a little boy.
-Joseph Heller

How sweet it is when the strong are also gentle!
-Libbie Fudim

The boy who is going to make a great man
must not make up his mind merely to overcome a
thousand obstacles, but to win in spite of a thousand
repulses and defeats.
-Theodore Roosevelt

It's not the men in my life, but the life in my men.
-Mae West

A boy is a magical creature – you can lock him out of your
workshop, but you can't lock him out of your heart.
-Alan Beck

Of all the unsettling, rough, crude,
living things found in the woods,
the most strange is the boy.
-Crystal Dawn Perry

I'm the kind of guy that can't keep a plant alive for a week,
let alone a relationship.
-Jerry O'Connell

Boys should abstain from all use of wine until
their eighteenth year, for it is wrong to add fire to fire.
-Plato

The glory of the nation rests in the character of her men.
And character comes from boyhood.
Thus every boy is a challenge to his elders.
-Herbert Hoover

Braces

Three stages in a parent's life: Nutrition, Dentition, Tuition
-Marcelene Cox

You can sit there with your mouth shut
or you can smile and brighten the world.
-Crystal Dawn Perry

...there shall be weeping and gnashing of teeth.
-Matthew 8:12 KJV

Break-up
(see also Friends-Long Distance and Memories)

We were together. I have forgotten the rest.
-Walt Whitman

There are better things ahead than any we leave behind.
-C.S. Henry Lewis

The greater your capacity to love,
the greater your capacity to feel the pain.
-Jennifer Anniston

If love is the answer,
could you please rephrase the question?
-Lily Tomlin

The magic of first love is our ignorance that it can ever end.
-Benjamin Disraeli

I'm the kind of guy that can't keep
a plant alive for a week, let alone a relationship.
-Jerry O'Connell

Romance fails us – and so do friendships –
but the relationship of Mother and Child
remains indelible and indestructible –
the strongest bond upon this earth.
-Theodore Reik

Heartbreak is life educating us.
-George Bernard Shaw

The best way to mend a broken heart
is time and girlfriends.
-Gwyneth Paltrow

In three words I can sum up everything
I've learned about life-
It goes on.
-Robert Frost

Brother
(See also Family/Heritage and Sibling)

That all men should be brothers
is the dream of people who have no brothers.
-Charles Chincholles

As I have discovered by examining my past,
I started out as a child. Coincidentally, so did my brother...
who taught me what was meant by "survival of the fittest."
-Bill Cosby

A brother is a friend given by nature.
-Jean Baptiste Legouve

Big Brother is watching you.
-George Orwell

We must learn to live together as brothers
or perish together as fools.
-Martin Luther King, Jr.

We few. We happy few. We band of brothers.
-William Shakespeare

If you want to know how your girl will treat you...
just listen to her talking to her little brother.
-Sam Levenson

Why the extra "r" in bother?
-Crystal Dawn Perry

You don't live in a world all alone.
Your brothers are here too.
-Albert Schweitzer

He ain't heavy, he's my brother.
-Neil Diamond

There is a destiny which makes us brothers.
None goes his way alone.
-Edwin Markham

How good and pleasant it is
when brothers live together in unity!
-Psalm 133:1 (NIV)

Camping
(see also Nature and Off-road)

Yesterday is ashes; tomorrow wood.
Only today does the fire burn brightly.
-Eskimo Saying

Of all the unsettling, rough, crude,
living things found in the woods,
the most strange is the boy.
-Crystal Dawn Perry

Car/Driving

Everything in life is somewhere else-
and you get there in a car.
-Elwyn Brooks White

American youth attributes much more importance to
arriving at driver's license age than at voting age.
-Marshall McLuhan

A good friend is a connection to life -
a tie to the past, a road to the future,
the key to sanity in a totally insane world.
-Lois Wyse

Oh! The places you'll go!
-Dr. Seuss

When looking down the road to see where you're going,
take time to notice the people
who are there beside you now.
-Crystal Dawn Perry

Never lend your car to anyone
to whom you have given birth.
-Erma Bombeck

You know your children are growing up
when they stop asking where they came from
and refuse to tell you where they're going.
-P.J. O'Rourke

The Write TEEN Words

The best way to keep children home is to make the home
atmosphere pleasant – and let the air out of the tires.
-Dorothy Parker

A suburban mother's role is to deliver children
obstetrically once, and by car ever after.
-Peter de Vries

A teenager who learns from his grandfather how much
gasoline a dollar used to buy must feel pretty discouraged.
-Phil Scott

Never invest your money in anything
that eats or needs repairing.
-Billy Rose

As we drive along this road of life, occasionally
a gal will find herself a little lost; and when that happens,
I guess she has to let go of the coulda, shoulda, woulda,
buckle up and just keep going.
-Sarah Jessica Parker

I may not have gone where I intended to go,
but I think I ended up where I intended to be.
-Douglas Adams

Let us go singing far as we go; the road will be less tedious.
-Virgil

A teenager out of sight is like a kite in the clouds;
even though you can't see it you feel the tug on the string.
-Marcelene Cox

The wrecks of matter and the crush of worlds.
-Joseph Addison

The longest journey begins with a single step,
not with a turn of the ignition key.
-Edward Abbey

Automobiles are not ferocious....
it is man who is to be feared.
-Robbins B. Stoeckel

Have you ever noticed? Anybody going slower than you is an idiot, and anyone going faster than you is a maniac.
-Ronnie Corbett

Cat
(see also Animal/Pet)

If cats could talk, they wouldn't.
-Nan Porter

Some people say that cats are sneaky, evil, and cruel. True, and they have many other fine qualities as well.
-Missy Dizick

There is something about the presence of a cat... that seems to take the bite out of being alone.
-Louis J. Camuti

Time spent with cats is never wasted.
-Colette

In ancient times cats were worshipped as gods; they have not forgotten this.
-Terry Pratchett

Character/Personality Traits
(see also Attitude, Beauty, Ego and Fun/Silliness)

What is right for one soul may not be right for another. It may mean having to stand on your own and do something strange in the eyes of others.
-Eileen Caddy

If you ask me what I came into this world to do, I will tell you; I came to live out loud.
-Emila Zola

I am better than my reputation.
-Friedrich von Schiller

I think once you figure out who you are and what you love about yourself, it all kinda falls into place.
-Jennifer Anniston

You have a unique message to deliver,
a unique song to sing, a unique act of love to bestow.
This message, this song, and this act of love
have been entrusted exclusively to the one and only you.
-John Powell, S.J.

Charm is a way of getting the answer "yes"
without having asked any clear question.
-Albert Camus

The way you overcome shyness is to become so wrapped
up in something that you forget to be afraid.
-Lady Bird Johnson

"Why not?" is a slogan for an interesting life.
-Mason Cooley

"Be yourself!"
is about the worst advice you can give to some people.
-Tom Masson

Happiness is inward and not outward;
and so it does not depend on
what we have but on what we are.
-Henry Van Dyke

Enthusiasm is a divine possession.
-Margaret E. Sangster

How sweet it is when the strong are also gentle!
-Libbie Fudim

To be alone is to be different. To be different is to be alone.
-Suzanne Gordon

It's important that people should know what you stand for.
It's equally important that they know
what you won't stand for.
-Mary H. Waldrip

Life is a paradise for those who love
many things with a passion.
-Leo Buscaglia

I'm certainly not denying that I'm young, but I'm not fluff.
-Jessica Simpson

...a wise and discerning heart so that there will never have been anyone like you, nor will there ever be.
-1 Kings 3:12 NIV

Cheerleading
(See also Gymnastics, Sports/Games and Talent)

Cheerfulness and contentment are great beautifiers and are famous preservers of good looks.
-Charles Dickens

Cheerleading is an uplifting experience... lifting spirits, lifting voices, rising to the occasion, lifting other cheerleaders and getting a rise out of others.
-Crystal Dawn Perry

If you ask me what I came into this world to do, I will tell you; I came to live out loud.
-Emila Zola

Do not trust the cheering, for those persons would shout as much if you or I were going to be hanged.
-Oliver Cromwell

The best way to cheer yourself up is to try to cheer someone else up.
-Mark Twain

Child
(See Teenager)

Chores

A perfect summer day is when the sun is shining, the breeze is blowing, the birds are singing, and the lawn mower is broken.
-James Dent

Nothing is really work unless
you would rather be doing something else.
-James Matthew Barrie

Never put off 'til tomorrow what can be
put off 'til the day after tomorrow
-Robert Sweatman

Being born is like being kidnapped.
And then sold into slavery.
-Andy Warhol

There are no menial jobs, only menial attitudes.
-William J. Bennett

There are three ways to get something done;
do it yourself, hire someone, or forbid your kids to do it.
-Monta Crane

I always thought a yard was three feet...
then I started mowing the lawn.
-C.E. Cowman

If you want your children to keep their feet on the ground,
put some responsibility on their shoulders.
-Abigail Van Buren

Christmas
(See also Gift and Tradition)

The most vivid memories of Christmases past are usually
not of gifts given or received, but of the spirit of love,
the special warmth of Christmas worship,
the cherished little habits of home.
-Lois Rand

Christmas waves a magic wand over this world,
and behold, everything is softer and more beautiful.
-Norman Vincent Peale

More than Santa Claus,
your sister knows when you've been bad or good.
-Linda Sunshine

It is Christmas in the heart that puts Christmas in the air.
-W.T. Ellis

"Bah," said Scrooge. "Humbug!"
-Charles Dickens

Love's the thing. The rest is tinsel.
-Pam Brown

Glory to God in the highest, and on earth
peace, good will toward men.
-St. Luke 2:14 KJV

Clothes
(See Shopping and Style)

Clubs/Committee/Leadership
(See also Talent)

Delegating work works,
provided the one delegating works, too.
-Robert Half

That's what being young is all about.
You have the courage and daring to think
that you can make a difference.
-Ruby Dee

I suppose leadership at one time meant muscles;
But today it means getting along with people.
-Indira Gandhi

A leader takes people where they want to go.
A great leader takes people where they don't
necessarily want to go but ought to be.
-Rosalynn Carter

It's important that people should know what you stand for.
It's equally important that they know
what you won't stand for.
-Mary H. Waldrip

The Write TEEN Words

I don't care to belong
to any club that will have me as a member.
-Groucho Marx

The only way to get something done is to do it.
-Crystal Dawn Perry

A president's hardest task is not to do what's right,
but to know what's right.
-Lyndon B. Johnson

The way you overcome shyness is to become
so wrapped up in something that you forget to be afraid.
-Lady Bird Johnson

College
(see also Independence and School)

You can lead a boy to college,
but you cannot make him think.
-Elbert Hubbard

Parents send their children to college either
because they went to college, or because they didn't.
-L.L. Henderson

The only qualification for admission was the ability
actually to find the campus
and then discover a parking space.
-Malcolm Bradbury

Does it seem impossible that the child will grow up?
That the bashful smile will become a bold expression...
that a briefcase will replace the blue security blanket?
-Anne Beattie

I'm going to college.
I don't care if it ruins my career.
-Natalie Portman

Three stages in a parent's life:
Nutrition, Dentition, Tuition
-Marcelene Cox

Get all the education you can,
but then, by God, do something.
Don't just stand there; make it happen.
-Lee Iococca

Computer

We've heard that a million monkeys at a million keyboards
could produce the complete works of Shakespeare;
now thanks to the Internet, we know that is not true.
-Robert Wilensky

Technology is a way of organizing the universe
so that man doesn't have to experience it.
-Max Frisch

The best thing about e-mail is
it has kept many people in touch.
The worst thing about e-mail is
it has kept many people in touch only by e-mail.
-Crystal Dawn Perry

The 'net is a waste of time
and that's exactly what's right about it.
-William Gibson

To err is human but to really foul things up
requires a computer.
-Farmer's Almanac

Letters from absent friends extinguish fear,
unite division, and draw distance near.
-Aaron Hill

My favorite thing about the Internet
is that you get to go into the private world of real creeps
without having to smell them.
-Penn Jillette

Cousin
(see Family/Heritage)

Dance
(see also Music and Talent)

If I could tell you what I mean,
there would be no point in dancing.
-Isadora Duncan

We're fools whether we dance or not,
so we might as well dance.
-Japanese Proverb

If you can walk, you can dance.
-Zimbabwe Saying

I am an onlooker on my daughter's dance.
Whenever she takes a pause and needs someone to talk to,
I am there; but that special dance
with the child and the future is hers.
-Liv Ullman

If I had my life to live over, I would start barefoot
earlier in the summer and stay that way later in the fall.
I would go to more dances.
I would ride more merry-go-rounds.
-Nadine Stair

Of two sisters one is always the watcher; one is the dancer.
-Louise Gluck

When you're skating on thin ice,
you may as well tap-dance.
-Bryce Courtenay

Dancing is like dreaming with your feet.
-Constanze

Dating
(see also Love)

Meeting someone for the first time is like going on
a treasure hunt. What wonderful worlds
we can find in others!
-Edward E. Ford

Our brightest blazes are commonly kindled
by unexpected sparks.
-Samuel Johnson

To get to a woman's heart, a man must first use his own.
-Mike Dobbertin

Say it with flowers.
-Patrick F. O'Keefe

The longer the wait, the better the date.
-Myriad Sky

I dreamed of it. I lived it. Now I relive it in my dreams.
-Crystal Dawn Perry

I don't have a boyfriend. I am an independent woman!
-Britney Spears

I have a lot of boyfriends. And I kiss them all!
-Ann Kournikova

I don't have a girlfriend;
but I do know a woman who'd be mad at me for saying that.
-Mitch Hedberg

From small beginnings come great things.
-Dutch proverb

Many a man wishes he were strong enough
to tear a telephone book in half —
especially if he has a teenage daughter.
-Guy Lombardo

He that would the daughter win,
must with the mother first begin.
-English proverb

Boys will be boys. And even that wouldn't matter
if only we could prevent girls from being girls.
-Anthony Hope Hawkins

A youth with his first cigar makes himself sick;
a youth with his first girl makes everybody sick.
-Mary Wilson Little

Right now I'm pretty single.
-Christina Aguilera

There are so many girls and so few princes.
-Liza Minelli

Daughter
(See also Family/Heritage, Girls and Teenager)

Who can describe the transports of a heart truly parental on beholding a daughter shoot up like some fair and modest flower, and acquire, day after day, fresh beauty and growing sweetness, so as to fill every eye with pleasure and every heart with admiration.
-James Fordyce

We are together, my child and I, Mother and child, yes, but sisters really, against whatever denies us all that we are.
-Alice Walker

I would say, "You might encounter defeats
but you must never be defeated."
I would teach her to love a lot,
laugh at the silliest things and be very serious.
I would teach her to love life.
-Maya Angelou

I am an onlooker on my daughter's dance.
Whenever she takes a pause and needs someone to talk to,
I am there; but that special dance
with the child and the future is hers.
-Liv Ullman

Many a man wishes he were strong enough
to tear a telephone book in half –
especially if he has a teenage daughter.
-Guy Lombardo

A daughter reminds you of all the things
you had forgotten about being young. Good and bad.
-Maeve O'Reily

Flowers o' the home are daughters.
-Marceline Desbordes-Valmore

There's something like a line of gold thread running through a man's words when he talks to his daughter, and gradually over the years it gets to be long enough for you to pick up in your hands and weave into a cloth that feels like love itself.
-John Gregory Brown

What I most wanted for my daughter was that she be able to soar confidently in her own sky, wherever that might be, and if there was space for me as well I would, indeed, have reaped what I had tried to sow.
-Helen Claes

Diet

Thin people are beautiful but fat people are adorable.
-Jackie Gleason

My therapist told me the way to achieve true inner peace is to finish what I start. So far today, I have finished two bags of M and M's and a chocolate cake. I feel better already.
-Dave Barry

Friendships come in many sizes and ours is extra-large.
-Unknown

Never eat more than you can lift.
-Miss Piggy

The body never lies.
-Martha Graham

Discipline/Grounding
(see Trouble)

Dog
(see also Animal/Pet)

Know yourself. Don't accept your dog's admiration
as conclusive evidence that you are wonderful.
-Ann Landers

My little dog... a heartbeat at my feet.
-Edith Wharton

Dogs are not our whole life, but they make our lives whole.
-Roger Caras

Dogs laugh...they laugh with their tails.
-Max Eastman

What matters is not the size of the dog in the fight,
but the size of the fight in the dog.
-Coach Bear Bryant

The great pleasure of a dog is that you may make a fool of
yourself with him and not only will he not scold you,
but he will make a fool of himself too.
-Samuel Butler

Do-it-yourself/Handiwork
(see also Arts/Crafts and Talent)

Life is a do-it-yourself project.
-Napoleon Hill

The ark was built by amateurs and the Titanic by experts.
Don't wait for the experts.
-Murray Cohen

There are three ways to get something done;
do it yourself, hire someone, or forbid your kids to do it.
-Monta Crane

The first rule of intelligent tinkering is to save all the parts.
-Paul R. Ehrlich

Many hands make light work.
-John Heywood

Duct tape is like the force. It has a light side, a dark side,
and it holds the universe together.
-Oprah Winfrey

Don't reinvent the wheel- just realign it.
-Anthony J. D'Angelo

A boy is a magical creature –
you can lock him out of your workshop,
but you can't lock him out of your heart.
-Alan Beck

Drama/School Program
(see also Talent)

Drama is life with the dull bits cut out.
-Alfred Hitchcock

We are all of us stars and we all deserve to twinkle.
-Marilyn Monroe

There are always three speeches
for every one you actually gave:
The one you practiced, the one you gave,
and the one you wish you gave.
-Dale Carnegie

If you ask me what I came into this world to do,
I will tell you; I came to live out loud.
-Emila Zola

I have the stardom glow.
-Jennifer Lopez

Nothing is more fascinating or theatrical than real life.
-Debra Messing

When words leave off, music begins.
-Heinrich Heine

The way you overcome shyness is to become
so wrapped up in something that you forget to be afraid.
-Lady Bird Johnson

Dreams/Goals/Ambition

Shoot for the moon.
Even if you miss, you'll land among the stars.
-Les Brown

I wish you so much.
But most of all, I wish you to be your own true self.
To take all the gifts that you were born with and make of them marvels of beauty and ingenuity and astonishment.
-Pam Brown

Never forget to dream.
-Madonna

The greatest dreams are always unrealistic.
-Will Smith

Friends…they cherish one another's hopes.
They are kind to one another's dreams.
-Henry David Thoreau

When I look into my future, it's so bright it burns my eyes.
-Oprah Winfrey

Some day they will know what I mean.
-Tom Thomson

The purpose of life is a life of purpose.
-Robert Byrne

All it takes is just one person telling me I can't do it and I'll use the fear of failure as fuel.
-Will Smith

Don't let anyone steal your dream.
It's your dream, not theirs.
-Dan Zadra

The only way to get something done is to do it.
-Crystal Dawn Perry

We are all in the gutter,
but some of us are looking at the stars.
-Oscar Wilde

Trust in God and do something.
-Mary Lyon

Dream as if you'll live forever. Live as if you'll die today.
-James Dean

Throw your dreams into space like a kite,
and you do not know what it will bring back, a new life,
a new friend, a new love, a new country.
-Anais Nin

My mother wanted me to be her wings, to fly as she
never quite had the courage to do. I love her for that.
I love the fact that she wanted to give birth to her own wings.
-Erica Jong

One can never consent to creep
when one feels an impulse to soar.
-Helen Keller

Easter
(see also Tradition)

Blue skies with white clouds on summer days.
A myriad of stars on clear moonlit nights, bluebirds,
and laughter and sunshine and Easter.
See how He loves us!
-Alice Chaplin

Spring bursts today, for Christ is risen
and all the earth's at play.
-Christina G. Rossetti

Put all thine eggs in one basket - and watch that basket.
-Mark Twain

'Twas Easter Sunday.
The full-blossomed trees filled all the air
with fragrance and with joy.
-Henry Wadsworth Longfellow

Exchange Student
(see also Friends-long distance)

I always try to teach by example...one of the reasons we're here is to be a part of this process of exchange.
-Dizzy Gillespie

Each friend represents a world in us,
a world not born before they arrive,
and it is only by this meeting that a new world is born.
-Anais Nin

Where I was born and where and how I have lived is unimportant. It is what I have done with where I have been that should be of interest.
-Georgia O'Keefe

Excitement/Extreme Sports/Fear

Life is either a daring adventure or nothing at all.
-Helen Keller

Feel the fear, and do it anyway.
-Susan Jeffers

I'll get there alive even if it kills me.
-Homer Simpson

All it takes is just one person telling me I can't do it and I'll use the fear of failure as fuel.
-Will Smith

"Why not?" is a slogan for an interesting life.
-Mason Cooley

Have a blast while you last.
-Hollis Stacy

If you ask me what I came into this world to do, I will tell you; I came to live out loud.
-Emila Zola

If you surrendered to the air, you could ride it.
-Toni Morrison

If all my friends were to jump off a cliff,
I wouldn't jump with them;
I'd be at the bottom to catch them.
-Tim McGraw

Son: acronym for Scared Of Nothing.
-Crystal Dawn Perry

The only thing we have to fear is fear itself.
-Franklin D. Roosevelt

Life is full of risks anyway, why not take them?
-Lindsay Lohan

I don't want to get to the end of my life
and find that I lived just the length of it.
I want to have lived the width of it as well.
-Diane Ackerman

Life is a great big canvas; throw all the paint on it you can.
-Danny Kaye

Dream as if you'll live forever.
Live as if you'll die today.
-James Dean

Exercise/Physique

Life is not so bad if you have plenty of luck,
a good physique and not too much imagination.
-Christopher Isherwood

Never eat more than you can lift.
-Miss Piggy

Nature makes boys and girls lovely to look upon
so they can be tolerated until they acquire some sense.
-William Lyon Phelps

It is only shallow people who do not judge by appearances.
-Oscar Wilde

Thin people are beautiful but fat people are adorable.
-Jackie Gleason

The body never lies.
-Martha Graham

Face
(see also Beauty)

For news of the heart, ask the face.
-Guinean proverb

Four be the things I'd have been better without:
Love, curiosity, freckles, and doubt.
-Dorothy Parker

A dimple in the chin; a devil within.
-Irish proverb

The eye is the jewel of the body.
-Henry David Thoreau

Family/Heritage

Heredity: An omnibus in which all our ancestors ride,
and every now and then, one of them
puts his head out and embarrasses us.
-Oliver Wendell Holmes

Family is just accident.
They don't mean to get on your nerves.
They don't even mean to be your family, they just are.
-Marsha Norman

Heredity is what sets the parents of a teenager
wondering about each other.
-Dr. Laurence J. Peter

Call it a clan, call it a network, call it a tribe, call it a family.
Whatever you call it, whoever you are, you need one.
-Jane Howard

Children in a family are like flowers in a bouquet;
there's always one determined to face in an opposite direction
from the way the arranger desires.
-Marcelene Cox

Remember... as far as anyone knows,
we're a nice normal family.
-Homer Simpson

I think a dysfunctional family is any family
with more than one person in it.
-Mary Karr

The problem with the gene pool is that there's no lifeguard.
-David Gerrold

Families are about love overcoming emotional torture.
-Matt Groening

A cousin is like having an arranged friendship.
-Crystal Dawn Perry

Insanity is hereditary; you can get it from your children.
-Sam Levinson

When you look at your life,
the greatest happinesses are family happinesses.
-Dr. Joyce Brothers

To forget one's ancestors
is to be a brook with a source, a tree without a root.
-Chinese proverb

God gives us our relatives—
thank God we can choose our friends.
-Ethel Watts Mumford

Having a family is like having
a bowling alley installed in your brain.
-Martin Mull

The family... We were a strange little band of characters
trudging through life sharing diseases and toothpaste,
coveting one another's desserts, hiding shampoo,
borrowing money, locking each other out of our rooms,
inflicting pain and kissing to heal it in the same instant,
loving, laughing, defending, and trying to figure out
the common thread that bound us all together.
-Erma Bombeck

A family is a unit composed not only of children,
but of fathers, mothers, an occasional animal and at times,
the common cold.
-Ogden Nash

Father
(See also Family/Heritage, Parent and Parent/Child Relationship)

The most important thing a father can do
for his children is to love their mother.
-Theodore M. Hesburgh

My father didn't tell me how to live;
he lived, and let me watch him do it.
-Clarence Budington Kelland

Love and fear...
everything the father of a family says
must inspire one or the other.
-Joseph Joubert

Many a man wishes he were strong enough
to tear a telephone book in half –
especially if he has a teenage daughter.
-Guy Lombardo

A father is a banker provided by nature.
-French proverb

He who has daughters is always a shepherd.
-Old saying

It's a wonderful feeling when your father becomes
not a god but a man to you –
when he comes down from the mountain and you see
he's this man with weaknesses.
And you love him as this whole being, not as a figurehead.
-Robin Williams

Old as she was, she still missed her daddy sometimes.
-Gloria Gaynor

There's something like a line of gold thread running through
a man's words when he talks to his daughter, and
gradually over the years it gets to be long enough
for you to pick up in your hands and weave into a cloth
that feels like love itself.
-John Gregory Brown

When a father gives to his son, both laugh;
when a son gives to his father, both cry.
-William Shakespeare

He wants to live on through something –
and in his case, his masterpiece is his son.
-Arthur Miller

A man can never quite understand a boy,
even when he has been a boy.
-G.K. Chesterton

It is not flesh and blood but the heart
which makes us fathers and sons.
-Johann Schiller

There is nothing stronger in the world than gentleness.
-Han Suyin

Fishing
(see also Swimming/Water Sports)

There's a fine line between fishing
and standing on the shore like an idiot.
-Steven Wright

The fishing was good. It was the catching that was bad.
-A.K. Best

Teach a man to fish and he will fish for a day.
Teach a man to fish and he will eat for a lifetime.
-Chinese proverb

If fishing is a religion, fly-fishing is the high church.
-Tom Brokaw

Three-fourths of the Earth's surface is water,
and one-fourth is land. It is quite clear that the good Lord
intended us to spend triple the amount of time fishing
as taking care of the lawn.
-Chuck Clark

Football
(see also Sports/Games and Talent)

I say, if your knees aren't green by the end of the day,
you ought to seriously re-examine your life.
-Bill Watterson, Calvin & Hobbes

Most football players are temperamental.
That's 90 percent temper and 10 percent mental.
-Doug Plank

I threw him heavily to the ground on top of me.
-Mark Twain

Some people think football is a matter of life and death...
I can assure them, it is much more serious than that.
-Bill Shankly

Friends/Best Friend
(see also Multiples)

When just being together is more important
than what you do, you are with a friend.
-Stephanie James

We are each of us angels with only one wing,
and we can only fly by embracing one another.
-Luciano deCrescenzo

A good friend is a connection to life - a tie to the past,
a road to the future, the key to sanity in a totally insane world.
-Lois Wyse

Many friends in general; one in special.
-George Herbert

A friend is...
a whole lot of wonderful people rolled into one.
-Gayle Lawrence

Anything, everything, little or big
becomes an adventure when the right person shares it.
-Kathleen Norris

1 out of 4 people in this country is mentally unbalanced.
Think of your three closest friends;
if they seem o.k., then you're the one.
-Ann Landers

Laughter is the shortest distance between two people.
-Victor Borge

My friendships are my life.
-Jodie Foster

A real friend is one who walks in
when the rest of the world walks out.
-Walter Winchell

Couples often share a special song;
friends share a special place.
-Crystal Dawn Perry

Friends aren't any more important
than breath or blood to a high school senior.
-Betty Ford

"Friendship," said Pooh, "is a very comforting sort of thing."
A.A. Milne

A friend is a second self.
-Aristotle

There are three kinds of friends:
best friends, guest friends, and pest friends.
-Laurence J. Peter

We have been friends together in sunshine and in shade.
-Caroline Sheridan Norton

The Write TEEN Words

God gives us our relatives—
thank God we can choose our friends.
-Ethel Watts Mumford

Friends will not only live in harmony, but in melody.
-Henry David Thoreau

The young always have the same problem –
how to rebel and conform at the same time.
They have now solved this by defying their elders
and copying one another.
-Quentin Crisp

Each friend represents a world in us,
a world not born before they arrive,
and it is only by this meeting that a new world is born.
-Anais Nin

A friend is a gift you give yourself.
-Robert Lewis Stevenson

Remember, the greatest gift is not found
in a store nor under a tree, but in the hearts of true friends.
-Cindy Lew

If all my friends were to jump off a cliff,
I wouldn't jump with them; I'd be at the bottom to catch them.
-Tim McGraw

Romance fails us – and so do friendships –
but the relationship of Mother and Child remains indelible
and indestructible– the strongest bond upon this earth.
-Theodore Reik

An aware parent loves all children he or she meets and
interacts with-for you are a caretaker
for those moments in time.
-Doc Childre

A friend is someone who knows all about you
and loves you just the same.
-Elbert Hubbard

Friends-long distance

We all take different paths in life
but no matter where we go,
we take a little of each other everywhere.
-Tim McGraw

Never shall I forget the time I spent with you.
Please continue to be my friend,
as you will always find me yours.
-Ludwig Van Beethoven

We were together. I have forgotten the rest.
-Walt Whitman

There are things that we never want to let go of,
people we never want to leave behind,
but keep in mind that letting go isn't the end of the world,
it's the beginning of a new life.
-Unknown

Never forget me...
because if I thought you would, I'd never leave.
-A.A. Milne

"Stay" is a charming word in a friend's vocabulary.
-Amos Bronson Alcott

Letters from absent friends extinguish fear,
unite division, and draw distance near.
-Aaron Hill

Absence makes the heart grow fonder.
-Thomas Haynes Bayly

The most beautiful discovery true friends make
is that they can grow separately without growing apart.
-Elisabeth Foley

Fun/Silliness

A normal adolescent isn't a normal adolescent
if he acts normal.
-Judith Viorst

When you're young,
the silliest notions seem the greatest achievements.
-Pearl Bailey

I am only young once- who cares if I'm a goofball!
-Ashton Kutcher

As long as I continue to hear "normal" people
telling me I am too childish, I know I'm doing just fine.
-Wayne Dyer

I pretty much try to stay in a constant state of confusion
just because of the expression it leaves on my face.
-Johnny Depp

Looks like some carnival lost a good act.
-James Gleason

1 out of 4 people in this country is mentally unbalanced.
Think of your three closest friends;
if they seem o.k., then you're the one.
-Ann Landers

Only two things are infinite,
the universe and human stupidity,
and I'm not sure about the former.
-Albert Einstein

Have a blast while you last.
-Hollis Stacy

Fun is good.
-Dr. Suess

Laughter is the shortest distance between two people.
-Victor Borge

Laughter and crying are twin experiences.
-Ai Bei

Think sideways!
-Edward de Bono

Love is being stupid together.
-Paul Valery

Insanity is hereditary; you can get it from your children.
-Sam Levenson

Life's better when it's fun. Boy, that's deep, isn't it?
-Kevin Costner

I don't think you should make fun of anyone but yourself.
-Cameron Diaz

Games
(see Sports/Games)

Gift

Memories are perhaps the best gifts of all.
-Gloria Gaither

May no gift be too small to give, nor too simple to receive,
which is wrapped in thoughtfulness and tied with love.
-L.O. Baird

A friend is a gift you give yourself.
-Robert Lewis Stevenson

Remember, the greatest gift is not found
in a store nor under a tree, but in the hearts of true friends.
-Cindy Lew

When a man is wrapped up in himself
he makes a pretty small package.
-John Ruskin

Changing a diaper is a lot like
getting a present from your grandmother –
you're not sure what you've got but
you're pretty sure you're not going to like it.
-Jeff Foxworthy

Every gift from a friend is a wish for your happiness.
-Richard Bach

Girls
(see also Teenager)

Girls we love for what they are;
young men for what they promise to be.
-Johann Wolfgang Von Goethe

Girls will be girls.
-Chinese proverb

Boys will be boys. And even that wouldn't matter
if only we could prevent girls from being girls.
-Anthony Hope Hawkins

I'm certainly not denying that I'm young, but I'm not fluff.
-Jessica Simpson

I am a woman in process.
-Oprah Winfrey

Anything boys can do, girls can do better...
and look more graceful doing it.
-Crystal Dawn Perry

A woman who looks like a girl and thinks like a man
is the best sort, the most enjoyable to be,
and the most pleasurable to have and to hold.
-Julie Burchill

The attributes of a great lady
may still be found in the rule of the four S's:
Sincerity, Simplicity, Sympathy, and Serenity.
-Emily Post

If school results were the key to power,
girls would be running the world.
-Sarah Boseley

What do girls do who haven't any mothers
to help them through their troubles?
-Louisa May Alcott

Every girl should use what Mother Nature gave her
before Father Time takes it away.
-Laurence J. Peter

There are so many girls, and so few princes.
-Liza Minelli

To grown people, a girl of fifteen and a half is a child still;
to herself, she is very old and very real,
perhaps, than ever before or after.
-Margaret Widdemer

Girlfriend
(see Dating and Love)

Glasses/Contacts
(also available: Sunglasses)

Now I see that I can see what I never saw.
-Crystal Dawn Perry

Competence, like truth, beauty and contact lenses,
is in the eye of the beholder.
-Laurence J. Peter

It's not what you look at that matters, it's what you see.
-Henry David Thoreau

Golf
(see also Sports/Games and Talent)

Life is like a golf swing.
Right here in the middle, where time flies by in seconds,
we have the opportunity to make decisions.
-David Meador

Go play golf. Go to the golf course.
Hit the ball. Find the ball.
Repeat until the ball is in the hole. Have fun. The end.
-Chuck Hogan

Golf is good for the soul.
You get so mad at yourself you forget to hate your enemies.
-Will Rogers

Don't forget to swing hard in case you hit the ball.
-Woodie Held

Graduation
(see also Dreams/Goals/Ambition)

There are better things ahead than any we leave behind.
-C.S. Lewis

The fireworks begin today.
Each diploma is a lighted match. Each one of you is a fuse.
-Edward Koch

The past cannot be regained, although we can learn from it;
the future is not yet ours even though we must plan for it...
Time is now. We have only today.
-Charles Hummell

The uncertainties of the present always give way
to the enchanted possibilities of the future.
-Gelsey Kirkland

All things must change to something new,
to something strange.
-Henry Wadsworth Longfellow

A graduation ceremony is an event where the
commencement speaker tells thousands of students
dressed in identical caps and gowns that "individuality"
is the key to success.
-Robert Orben

I'm set adrift, with a diploma for a sail
and lots of nerve for oars.
-Richard Halliburton

It is good to have an end to journey toward;
But it is the journey that matters, in the end.
-Ursula K. Le Guin

I may not have gone where I intended to go,
but I think I ended up where I intended to be.
-Douglas Adams

What lies behind us and what lies before us
are tiny matters compared to what lies within us.
-Ralph Waldo Emerson

Sooner or later we all discover that the important moments
in life are not the advertised ones, not the birthdays,
the graduations, the weddings, not the great goals achieved.
The real milestones are less prepossessing.
They come to the door of memory.
-Susan B. Anthony

"I know the plans I have for you," declares the Lord,
"plans to prosper you and not to harm you,
plans to give you hope and a future."
-Jeremiah 29:11 (NIV)

Grandchild/Grandparent
(see also Family/Heritage)

It is one of nature's ways that we often feel closer to distant
generations than to the generations
immediately preceding us.
-Igor Stravinsky

To the world, they are decades and miles apart
but to a grandparent, the grandchild is only a heartbeat away.
-Crystal Dawn Perry

Being grandparents sufficiently removes us from the
responsibilities so that we can be friends-
really good friends.
-Allan Frome

Beautiful young people are accidents of nature
but beautiful old people are works of art.
-Eleanor Roosevelt

In order to influence a child,
one must be careful not to be
that child's parent or grandparent.
-Don Marquis

The house with an old grandparent harbors a jewel.
-Chinese proverb

Every generation revolts against its fathers
and makes friends with its grandfathers.
-Lewis Mumford

Why do grandparents and grandchildren get along so well?
They have the same enemy- the mother.
-Claudette Colbert

Mothers of daughters
are daughters of mothers and have remained so,
in circles joined to circles, since time began.
-Signe Hammer

I'm a flower...opening and reaching for the sun.
You are the sun, Grandma, you are the sun in my life.
-Kitty Tsui

You've got to do your own growing,
no matter how tall your grandfather was.
-Irish proverb

Growing Up
(see also Everyday Moments and Independence)

So much of growing up is an unbearable waiting.
A constant longing for another time. Another season.
-Sonia Sanche

It is unjust to claim the privileges of age
and retain the playthings of childhood.
-Samuel Johnson

It will be gone before you know it.
The fingerprints on the wall appear higher and higher.
Then suddenly they disappear.
-Dorothy Evslin

Growth is the only evidence of life.
-Cardinal Newman

Once you do something really mature
there is no turning back.
-Lindsay Lohan

As you continue to grow
emotionally, spiritually, mentally and physically,
so does my love for you.
-Crystal Dawn Perry

Does it seem impossible that the child will grow up?
That the bashful smile will become a bold expression...
that a briefcase will replace the blue security blanket?
-Anne Beattie

Who can describe the transports of a heart truly parental
on beholding a daughter shoot up like some fair and
modest flower, and acquire, day after day, fresh beauty and
growing sweetness, so as to fill every eye with pleasure
and every heart with admiration.
-James Fordyce

Grown don't mean nothing to a mother. A child is a child.
They get bigger, older, but grown?
What's that suppose to mean?
In my heart it don't mean a thing.
-Toni Morrison

From small beginnings come great things.
-Proverb

Growing up happens in a heartbeat.
However, it is the longest, most difficult heartbeat of life.
-Crystal Dawn Perry

It kills you to see them grow up.
But I guess it would kill you quicker if they didn't.
-Barbara Kingsolver

You know your children are growing up
when they stop asking where they came from
and refuse to tell you where they're going.
-P.J. O'Rourke

If we don't change, we don't grow.
If we don't grow, we are not really living.
-Gail Sheehy

Gymnastics
(see also Sports/Games and Talent)

Better to bend than to break.
-French saying

Everybody knows if you are too careful you are so occupied in being careful that you are sure to stumble over something.
-Gertrude Stein

The world is wrong side up.
It needs to be turned upside down in order to be right.
-William A. Sunday

To relax, be flexible.
-Crystal Dawn Perry

Habit

The fixity of a habit
is generally in direct proportion to its absurdity.
-Marcel Proust

Habit is stronger than reason.
-George Santayana

What one loves in childhood stays in the heart forever.
-Mary Jo Putney

The chains of habit are generally too small to be felt until they are too strong to be broken.
-Samuel Johnson

Hair

A bad haircut is two people's shame.
-Danish proverb

A teenager is life's aspirations, doubts, mysteries, miseries,
and love, all wrapped up and tied together with unruly hair.
-Crystal Dawn Perry

I was sick of people making fun of my hair and so I cut it
off and I've got much more attention than ever before.
It was like when Mona Lisa was stolen
from the Louvre in 1906 –
three times more people came to see where it used to be.
-Emo Philips

Why don't you get a haircut;
You look like a chrysanthemum.
-P.G. Wodehouse

I'm not offended by all the dumb-blonde jokes because
I know that I'm not dumb. I also know I'm not blonde.
-Dolly Parton

Who is this porcupine that lives in my house,
eats my food, and talks back to me? I don't know,
but under his quills, he's hiding my son.
-Crystal Dawn Perry

No matter how perfect your mother thinks you are,
she will always want to fix your hair.
-Suzanne Beilenson

Half-Sibling
A human being is ...
one or the other half of an unsolved equation.
-Christopher Morley

I don't know half of you half as well as I should like;
and I like less than half of you half as well as you deserve.
-J.R.R. Tolkien

I believe one half of the world is born
for the convenience of the other half.
-Sarah Siddons

Halloween

A mask tells us more than a face.
-Oscar Wilde

Innocence itself sometimes hath need of a mask.
-Polish proverb

Double, double, toil and trouble.
-William Shakespeare

'Tis now the very witching time of night
when churchyards yawn.
-William Shakespeare

Handicap
(see Hardship and Special Needs)

Hang-out/Special Place

How hard it is to escape from places.
However carefully one goes, they hold you;
you leave little bits of yourself fluttering on the fences –
like rags and shreds of your very life.
-Katherine Mansfield

It isn't how much time you spend somewhere
that makes it memorable; it's how you spend the time.
-David Brenner

The time to be happy is now. The place to be happy is here.
-Robert G. Ingersoll

Couples often share a special song;
friends share a special place.
-Crystal Dawn Perry

Hanukkah

Hanukkah reminds us that faith
can give us the strength to overcome oppression.
-George H.W. Bush

Happiness

Recall it as often as you wish,
a happy memory never wears out.
-Libbie Fudim

Happiness is a butterfly which,
when pursued, is always just beyond your grasp, but which,
if you will sit down quietly, may alight upon you.
-Nathaniel Hawthorne

Where your pleasure is, there is your treasure;
where your treasure, there is your heart;
where your heart, there is your happiness.
-Augustine

Happiness is inward and not outward;
and so it does not depend on what we have
but on what we are.
-Henry Van Dyke

Happiness isn't getting what you want;
it's wanting what you got.
-Garth Brooks

Life itself is the most wonderful fairy tale.
-Hans Christian Andersen

The time to be happy is now. The place to be happy is here.
-Robert G. Ingersoll

Have a blast while you last.
-Hollis Stacy

When you look at your life,
the greatest happinesses are family happinesses.
-Dr. Joyce Brothers

The best way to cheer yourself up
is to try to cheer somebody else up.
-Mark Twain

The moments of happiness we enjoy take us by surprise.
It is not that we seize them, but that they seize us.
-Ashley Morgan Montagu

Happiness always looks small while you hold it in your hands,
but let it go, and you learn at once
how big and precious it is.
-Maxim Gorky

I was broke, but I was happy.
-Jennifer Garner

The Lord has done great things for us,
and we are filled with joy.
-Psalm 126:3 (NIV)

Hardship

Parents learn a lot from their children
about coping with life.
-Muriel Spark

I don't think of all the misery
but of the beauty that still remains.
-Anne Frank

Hope is a gift we give ourselves,
and it remains when all else is gone.
-Naomi Judd

If you're going through it, you can come out.
-Fantasia Barrino

Where there's life, there's hope.
-Terence

Little children, headache; big children, heartache.
-Italian Proverb

What does not destroy me, makes me strong.
-Friedrich Nietzsche

In three words I can sum up everything
I've learned about life...
It goes on.
-Robert Frost

Forgiving is all; forgetting is another thing.
-Bob Rae

Heartbreak is life educating us.
-George Bernard Shaw

Sadness flies away on the wings of time.
-Jean de La Fontaine

Hobby/Collection

A collection is memories and emotions,
held in the hand as well as the heart.
-Crystal Dawn Perry

What one loves in childhood stays in the heart forever.
-Mary Jo Putney

Life is a paradise for those who love
many things with a passion.
-Leo Buscaglia

There is a very fine line between
"hobby" and "mental illness."
-Dave Barry

Make the most of today. Get interested in something.
Shake yourself awake. Develop a hobby.
Let the winds of enthusiasm sweep through you.
Live today with gusto.
-Dale Carnegie

Hockey
(See also Skating, Sports/Games and Talent)

You miss 100% of the shots you don't take.
-Wayne Gretzky

I went to a fight the other day
and a hockey game broke out.
-Rodney Dangerfield

I skate to where the puck is going to be,
not where it has already been.
-Wayne Gretzky

A puck is a hard rubber disc that hockey players strike
when they can't hit one another.
-Jimmy Cannon

Big shots are only little shots who keep shooting.
-Christopher Morley

Home

Be it ever so humble, there's no place like home.
-John Howard Payne

Be grateful for the home you have,
knowing that at this moment, all you have is all you need.
-Sarah Ban Breathnach

Home is any four walls that enclose the right person.
-Helen Rowland

Ah! There is nothing like staying at home for real comfort.
-Jane Austen

Home...
where we begin, where we grow, where we always long for,
where the love is always a different love
than found anywhere else on earth.
-Crystal Dawn Perry

If your children spend most of their time
in other people's houses, you're lucky;
if they all congregate at your house, you're blessed.
-Mignon McLaughlin

Home is where the heart's tears can dry at their own pace.
-Vernon G. Baker

Where we love is home,
home that our feet may leave, but not our hearts.
-Oliver Wendell Holmes

A house divided cannot stand.
-Arabic proverb

Home School
(see also School)

One mother can achieve more than a hundred teachers.
-Jewish Proverb

The mother's heart is the child's schoolroom.
-Henry Ward Beecher

Parents teach in the toughest school in the world:
The School for Making People.
You are the board of education, the principal,
the classroom teacher, and the janitor.
-Virginia Satir

The family is the school of duties, founded on love.
-Felix Adler

Homecoming
(also available: Parade)

All now was turned to jollity and game,
to luxury and riot, feast and dance.
-John Milton

Homecoming: Game-going and a dance.
-Crystal Dawn Perry

Hope Chest

Faith is the very first thing you should pack in a hope chest.
-Sarah Ban Breathnach

Hug/Kiss

The best thing to hold onto in life is each other.
-Audrey Hepburn

Do not make me kiss, and you will not make me sin.
-Russian proverb

Hold me close, let me go.
-Adair Lara

For it was not into my ear you whispered, but into my
heart. It was not my lips you kissed, but my soul.
-Judy Garland

The love we give away is the only love we keep.
-Elbert Hubbard

There is nothing stronger in this world than gentleness.
-Han Suyin

To love and be loved is to feel the sun from both sides.
-David Viscott

He felt now that he was not simply close to her,
but that he did not know where he ended and she began.
-Leo Tolstoy

We are each of us angels with only one wing,
and we can only fly by embracing one another.
-Luciano deCrescenzo

Hunting

Big shots are only little shots who keep shooting.
-Christopher Morley

The buck stops here.
-Harry S. Truman

A hungry dog hunts best.
-Lee Trevino

I ask people why they have deer heads on their walls.
They always say because it's such a beautiful animal...
I think my mother is attractive
but I have photographs of her.
-Ellen DeGenerous

Hunting is not a sport.
In a sport, both sides should know they're in the game.
-Paul Rodriguez

Illness/Injury

A family is a unit composed not only of children, but of fathers, mothers, an occasional animal and at times, the common cold.
-Ogden Nash

Sticks and stones may break my bones, but words will never hurt me.
-American proverb

Life is not merely to be alive, but to be well.
-Marcus Valerius Martial

Being sick is no fun but I sure like the attention!
-Carl Joseph Vonnoh, III

There are some remedies worse than the disease.
-Publilius Syrus

Fall sick and you will see who is your friend and who is not.
-Spanish proverb

Warning: Humor may be hazardous to your illness.
-Ellie Katz

If I die, I forgive you; if I recover, we shall see.
-Spanish proverb

He that courts injury will obtain it.
-Danish proverb

'Tis easier to hurt than heal.
-German proverb

Woe is me for my hurt!
-Jeremiah 10:19 KJV

Independence

What I most wanted for my daughter was that she be able to soar confidently in her own sky, wherever that might be, and if there was space for me as well I would, indeed, have reaped what I had tried to sow.
-Helen Claes

No bird soars too high if he soars with his own wings.
-William Blake

There are only two lasting bequests we can hope to give
our children. One of these is roots, the other, wings.
-Hodding Carter

I am not you anymore;
I am my own collection of gifts and errors.
-Saundra Sharp

It is harder to come back than to leave from here.
-Natasha Fuller

Where we love is home,
home that our feet may leave, but not our hearts.
-Oliver Wendell Holmes

Sometimes in your life you will go on a journey.
It will be the longest journey you have ever taken.
It is the journey to find yourself.
-Katherine Sharp

"Just living is not enough," said the butterfly.
"One must have sunshine, freedom, and a little flower."
-Hans Christian Andersen

A teenager out of sight is like a kite in the clouds;
even though you can't see it, you feel the tug on the string.
-Marcelene Cox

We have all been placed on this earth
to discover our own path,
and we will never be happy
if we live someone else's idea of life.
-James Van Praagh

People say that you're going the wrong way
when it's simply a way of your own.
-Angelina Jolie

Human beings are the only creatures
that allow their children to come back home.
-Bill Cosby

Give curiosity freedom.
-Eudora Welty

Hold me close, let me go.
-Adair Lara

A mother never realizes
that her children are no longer children.
-Holbrook Jackson

Independence Day

If there is a more optimistic holiday than July Fourth,
I don't know what it is; the food, the spectacle, the picnics,
the reminder that there are still a delicious nine weeks
left until the end of summer.
-Betsy Carter

I was born an American.
I will live an American;
I shall die an American.
-Daniel Webster

You're a grand old flag.
You're a high flying flag;
and forever in peace may you wave.
-George M. Cohan

Independence now; and Independence forever.
-Daniel Webster

Job
(see Work)

Laziness

Never put off 'til tomorrow
what can be put off 'til the day after tomorrow
-Robert Sweatman

Growth is the only evidence of life.
-Cardinal Newman

A sobering thought:
What if, right at this very moment,
I am living up to my full potential?
-Jane Wagner

If you can spend a perfectly useless afternoon
in a perfectly useless manner, you have learned how to live.
-Lin Yutang

I don't have anything against work.
I just figure why deprive somebody who really loves it?
-Dobie Gillis

The time you enjoy wasting is not wasted time.
-Bertrand Russell

Life/Everyday Moments

Life is either a daring adventure or nothing at all.
-Helen Keller

Life is a great big canvas; throw all the paint on it you can.
-Danny Kaye

Life is about not knowing, having to change,
taking the moment and making the best of it,
without knowing what's going to happen next.
-Gilda Radner

Life is not measured by the number of breaths we take
but by the moments that take our breath away.
-George Carlin

"Just living is not enough," said the butterfly.
"One must have sunshine, freedom, and a little flower."
-Hans Christian Andersen

I try to believe like I believed when I was five...
when your heart tells you everything you need to know.
-Lucy Liu

Write in your heart that every day
is the best day of the year.
-Ralph Waldo Emerson

The great duties of life are written with a sunbeam.
-John Jortin

The past cannot be regained, although we can learn from it; the future is not yet ours even though we must plan for it... Time is now. We have only today.
-Charles Hummell

Dream as if you'll live forever. Live as if you'll die today.
-James Dean

Life is a paradise for those who love many things with a passion.
-Leo Buscaglia

Have a blast while you last.
-Hollis Stacy

Life is ours to be spent, not to be saved.
-D.H. Lawrence

May you live all the days of your life.
-Jonathan Swift

As we drive along this road of life, occasionally a gal will find herself a little lost; and when that happens, I guess she has to let go of the coulda, shoulda, woulda, buckle up and just keep going.
-Sarah Jessica Parker

Life itself is the most wonderful fairytale.
-Hans Christian Andersen

We have all been placed on this earth to discover our own path, and we will never be happy if we live someone else's idea of life.
-James Van Praagh

I am I plus my circumstances.
-Jose Ortega y Gasset

Life's better when it's fun. Boy, that's deep, isn't it?
-Kevin Costner

Time is a very precious gift of God; so precious that it's only given to us moment by moment.
-Amelia Barr

To be nobody but yourself –
in a world which is doing its best, night and day,
to make you everybody else- means to fight the hardest
battle which any human being can fight,
and never stop fighting.
-E.E. Cummings

Life isn't a matter of milestones, but of moments.
-Rose Kennedy

Sooner or later we all discover that the important moments
in life are not the advertised ones, not the birthdays,
the graduations, the weddings,
not the great goals achieved.
The real milestones are less prepossessing.
They come to the door of memory.
-Susan B. Anthony

Happy times and bygone days are never lost... In truth,
they grow more wonderful within the heart that keeps them.
-Kay Andrews

We can only be said to be alive in those moments
when our hearts are conscious of our treasures.
-Thornton Wilder

How we spend our days is, of course,
how we spend our lives.
-Annie Dillard

Love
(see also Dating)

I know what love is. It's understanding.
It's you and me and let the rest of the world go by.
-Dewitt Bodeen

The best and most beautiful things in the world
cannot be seen or even touched.
They must be felt with the heart.
-Helen Keller

When you love someone,
all your saved up wishes start coming out.
-Elizabeth Bowen

The greater your capacity to love,
the greater your capacity to feel the pain.
-Jennifer Anniston

No one can understand love
who has not experienced infatuation.
And no one can understand infatuation,
no matter how many times he has experienced it.
-Mignon McLaughlin

Love...the heart's unbridled hope.
-Crystal Dawn Perry

We are all a little weird and life's a little weird,
and when we find someone whose weirdness
is compatible with ours, we join up with them
and fall in mutual weirdness and call it love.
-Robert Fulghum

Love is being stupid together.
-Paul Valery

All my soul follows you...and I live in being yours.
-Robert Browning

To love and be loved is to feel the sun from both sides.
-David Viscott

Do you love me because I'm beautiful,
or am I beautiful because you love me?
-Oscar Hammerstein, II

The magic of first love is our ignorance that it can ever end.
-Benjamin Disraeli

The logic of the heart is absurd.
-Julie de Lespinasse

Love doesn't make the world go 'round.
Love is what makes the ride worthwhile.
-Franklin P. Jones

The quickest way to receive love is to give;
the fastest way to lose love is to hold it too tightly;
and the best way to keep love is to give it wings.
-Brian Dyson

We loved with a love that was more than love.
-Edgar Allan Poe

He felt now that he was not simply close to her,
but that he did not know where he ended and she began.
-Leo Tolstoy

Love is a friendship set to music.
-E. Joseph Cossman

If I love you, what business is it of yours?
-Johann Wolfgang von Goethe

Make-up

Beauty to me is being comfortable in your own skin...
that, or red lipstick.
-Gwyneth Paltrow

My face looks like a wedding cake left out in the rain.
-W.H. Auden

There is no cosmetic for beauty like happiness.
-Lady Blessington

Martial Arts
(see also Sports/Games and Talent)

I am the Fred Astaire of karate.
-Jean Claude van Damme

To me, Judo is like a ballet, except there's no music,
no choreography, and the dancers knock each other down.
-Jack Handy

Take things as they are.
Punch when you have to punch. Kick when you have to kick.
-Bruce Lee

Memories

Recall it as often as you wish,
a happy memory never wears out.
-Libbie Fudim

Happiness always looks small
while you hold it in your hands, but let it go,
and you learn at once how big and precious it is.
-Maxim Gorky

Sadness flies away on the wings of time.
-Jean de La Fontaine

Happy times and bygone days are never lost...
In truth, they grow more wonderful
within the heart that keeps them.
-Kay Andrews

What we have once enjoyed we can never lose.
All that we love deeply becomes a part of us.
-Helen Keller

Memory is the diary that we all carry about with us.
-Oscar Wilde

You can clutch the past so tightly to your chest
that it leaves your arms too full to embrace the present.
-Jan Glidewell

Music is the way our memories sing to us across time.
-Lance Morrow

Sooner or later we all discover
that the important moments in life are not the advertised
ones, not the birthdays, the graduations, the weddings,
not the great goals achieved.
The real milestones are less prepossessing.
They come to the door of memory.
-Susan B. Anthony

Memory of a Loved One
(see also Memories)

To live in hearts we leave behind is not to die.
-Thomas Campbell

Life is not measured by the number of breaths we take
but by the moments that take our breath away.
-George Carlin

Be a life long or short,
its completeness depends on what it was lived for.
-David Starr Jordan

Whom the gods love dies young.
-Spanish proverb

We call that person who has lost his father,
an orphan; and a widower that man who has lost his wife.
But that man who has known the immense unhappiness
of losing a friend, by what name do we call him?
Here every language is silent
and holds its peace in impotence.
-Joseph Roux

She weeps for him a mother's burning tears-
She loved him with a mother's deepest love.
-Paul Laurence Dunbar

The longer one lives in this hard world motherless,
the more a mother's loss makes itself felt.
-Jane Welsh Carlyle

It's sad when our daddies die.
It makes us one less person inside.
-Pamela Ribon

We were together. I have forgotten the rest.
-Walt Whitman

Military

Throw your dreams into space like a kite,
and you do not know what it will bring back;
a new life, a new friend, a new love, a new country.
-Anais Nin

First in war, first in peace,
first in the hearts of his countrymen.
-Henry Leo

To have a son in wartime is the worst curse
that can befall a mother, no matter what anyone says.
-Slavenka Drakulic

Courage is resistance to fear, mastery of fear,
not absence of fear.
-Mark Twain

The glory of the nation rests in the character of her men.
And character comes from boyhood.
Thus every boy is a challenge to his elders.
-Herbert Hoover

There is many a boy here today who looks on war as all glory,
but boys, it is all hell.
-William Sherman

Independence now; and Independence forever.
-Daniel Webster

Money

It is frequently said that children do not know the value of money. This is only partially true. They do not know the value of your money. Their money, they know the value of.
-Judy Markey

Life is ours to be spent, not to be saved.
-D.H. Lawrence

I don't know much about being a millionaire,
but I'll bet I'd be darling at it.
-Dorothy Parker

If saving money is wrong, I don't want to be right!
-William Shatner

A father is a banker provided by nature.
-French proverb

Mother
(See also Family/Heritage, Parent and Parent/Child Relationship)

God could not be everywhere
and therefore he made mothers.
-Jewish proverb

My mother and I could always look out the same window
without ever seeing the same thing.
-Gloria Swanson

Romance fails us – and so do friendships –
but the relationship of Mother and Child
remains indelible and indestructible
– the strongest bond upon this earth.
-Theodore Reik

How simple a thing it seems to me that to know ourselves
as we are, we must know our mothers.
-Alice Walker

Yes, a mother is one thing that nobody can do without.
And when you have harassed her... tried her patience,
and worn her out, and it seems that the end of the world is
about to descend on you, then you can win her back
with four little words, "Mom, I love you."
-William A. Greenbaum II

Instant availability without continuous presence is
probably the best role a mother can play.
-Lotte Bailyn

The most important thing she's learned over the years
was that there was no way to be a perfect mother
and a million ways to be a good one.
-Jill Churchill

A mother starts out as the most important person
in her child's world and if she's successful in her work,
she will eventually become the stupidest.
-Mary Kay Blakely

My mother wanted me to be her wings, to fly as she never
quite had the courage to do. I love her for that.
I love the fact that she wanted to give birth to her own wings.
-Erica Jong

When you have a good mother and no father,
God kind of sits in. It's not enough, but it helps.
-Dick Gregory

What do girls do who haven't any mothers
to help them through their troubles?
-Louisa May Alcott

A suburban mother's role
is to deliver children obstetrically once,
and by car ever after.
-Peter de Vries

A mother's love endures through all.
-Washington Irving

Of all the rights of women, the greatest is to be a mother,
-Lin Yu-Tang

To describe my mother would be
to write about a hurricane in its perfect power.
-Maya Angelou

And it came to me, and I knew
what I had to have before my soul would rest.
I wanted to belong – to belong to my mother.
And in return – I wanted my mother to belong to me.
-Gloria Vanderbilt

Yes, Mother...I see that you are flawed.
You have not hidden it. That is your greatest gift to me.
-Alice Walker

Motorcycle

A mother is never cocky or proud,
because she knows the school principal
may call at any minute to report that her child has just
driven a motorcycle through the gymnasium.
-Mary Kay Blakely

There's all this language where you can't jump out of a plane
or ride motorcycles. You have to go home and just sit there.
-Ben Affleck

Movies/Television

Whoever controls the media - the images -
controls the culture.
-Allen Ginsberg

I find television very educational.
Every time someone turns on the set,
I go into the other room and read a book.
-Groucho Marx

If anything is poisoning our lives
and weakening our society, it is reality-
and not the fabrication of television writers and producers.
-Martin Maloney

Another possible source of guidance for teenagers is
television, but television's message has always been that
the need for truth, wisdom, and world peace pales by
comparison with the need for a toothpaste that offers
whiter teeth and fresher breath.
-Dave Barry

No form of art goes
beyond ordinary consciousness as film does;
Straight to our emotions,
deep into the twilight room of the soul.
-Ingmar Bergman

Television has changed the American child
from an irresistible force to an immovable object.
-Laurence J. Peter

Multiples
(see also Sibling)

Are we not like two volumes of one book?
-Marceline Desbordes-Valmore

We two form a multitude.
-Ovid

Double, double, toil and trouble.
-William Shakespeare

All who would win joy must share it;
happiness was born a twin.
-Lord Byron

Laughter and crying are twin experiences.
-Ai Bei

The love of beauty in its multiple forms is the noblest gift.
-Alexis Carrell

Music
(see also Band/Musical Instruments and Talent)

Friends will not only live in harmony, but in melody.
-Henry David Thoreau

Love is a friendship set to music.
-E. Joseph Cossman

If you ask me what I came into this world to do,
I will tell you; I came to live out loud.
-Emile Zola

Rock is all about writing your own script;
it's all about pioneering.
-Courtney Love

I celebrate myself, and sing myself.
-Walt Whitman

Music is the way our memories sing to us across time.
-Lance Morrow

You have a unique message to deliver,
a unique song to sing, a unique act of love to bestow.
This message, this song, and this act of love
have been entrusted exclusively to the one and only you.
-John Powell, S.J.

There are days when you don't have a song in your heart.
Sing anyway.
-Emory Austin

Let us go singing far as we go; the road will be less tedious.
-Virgil

Those who wish to sing, always find a song.
-Swedish proverb

My son does not appreciate classical musicians
such as the Stones; he is more into bands with names like
"Heave" and "Squatting Turnips."
-Dave Barry

Without music, life is a journey through a desert.
-Pat Conroy

Nature
(see also Off-road)

We all take different paths in life
but no matter where we go,
we take a little of each other everywhere.
-Tim McGraw

Live each day as you would climb a mountain...
Climb slowly, steadily, enjoying each passing moment;
And the view from the summit will serve
as a fitting climax for the journey.
-Harold V. Melchert

Nature is too thin a screen;
the glory of the omnipresent God bursts through everywhere.
-Ralph Waldo Emerson

Not all those who wander are lost.
-J.R.R. Tolkien

Nature never did betray the heart that loved her.
-William Wordsworth

Best friend, my wellspring in the wilderness!
-George Eliot

New Year

Now let us welcome the New Year...
full of things that have never been.
-Rainer Maria Rilke

Cheers to a new year and another chance for us to get it right.
-Oprah Winfrey

A new year can begin only because the old year ends.
-Madeleine L'Engle

Off-Road
(see also Nature)

Two roads diverged in a wood, and I-
I took the one less traveled by,
and that has made all the difference.
-Robert Frost

New roads; new ruts.
-G.K. Chesterton

No one should be able to enter
a wilderness by mechanical means.
-Garrett Hardin

Every path has its puddle.
-Old saying

Parade

And when it rains on your parade, look up rather than down.
Without the rain, there would be no rainbow.
-Jerry Chin

Hats off! Along the street there comes a blare of bugles,
a ruffle of drums, a flash of color beneath the sky;
Hats off! The flag is passing by.
-Henry Holcomb Bennett

Leadership involves finding a parade
and getting in front of it.
-John Neisbitt

Steps with a tender foot, light as on air,
the lovely, lordly creature floated on.
-Lord Alfred Tennyson

Parent
(See also Family/Heritage, Father, Mother, Parent/Child Relationship and Teenager)

Having one child makes you a parent;
having two or three makes you a referee.
-David Frost

Parents just don't understand.
-Will Smith

A wild goose never raised a tame gosling.
-Irish proverb

Adolescence is a period of rapid changes.
Between the ages of 12 and 17, for example,
a parent ages as much as 20 years.
-Al Bernstein

Part of the good part of being a parent
is a constant sense of deja vu.
But some of what you have to "vu"
you never want to "vu" again.
-Anna Quindlen

Are anybody's parents typical?
-Madeleine L'Engle

We are given children to test us and make us more spiritual.
-George Will

The joys of parents are secret,
and so are their griefs and fears.
-Francis Bacon

Parents are sometimes a bit of a disappointment to their children...they don't fulfill the promise of their early years.
-Anthony Powell

When looking down the road to see where you're going,
take time to notice the people who are there beside you now.
-Crystal Dawn Perry

Raising kids is part joy and part guerilla warfare.
-Ed Asner

It's not only children who grow. Parents do too.
As much as we watch to see what our children do with their lives, they are watching us to see what we do with ours.
I can't tell my children to reach for the sun.
All I can do is reach for it myself.
-Joyce Maynard

An aware parent loves all children
he or she meets and interacts with-
for you are a caretaker for those moments in time.
-Doc Childre

It's the biggest on-the-job training program
in existence today.
-Erma Bombeck

Let them know, no matter what, you will love them,
be proud of them, and furthermore, always be watching.
-Natasha Fuller

Life affords no greater responsibility,
no greater privilege, than the raising of the next generation.
-C. Everett Koop

Parent/Child Relationship
(See also Family/Heritage, Father, Mother, Parent and Teenager)

Children begin by loving their parents.
As they grow older they judge them,
sometimes they forgive them.
-Oscar Wilde

I am an onlooker on my daughter's dance.
Whenever she takes a pause and needs someone to talk to,
I am there; but that special dance
with the child and the future is hers.
-Liv Ullman

If you have never been hated by your child,
you have never been a parent.
-Bette Davis

In order to influence a child,
one must be careful not to be
that child's parent or grandparent.
-Don Marquis

Moments spent listening, talking,
playing, and sharing together
may be the most important times of all.
-Gloria Gaither

She discovered with great delight that one does not love
one's children just because they are one's children
but because of the friendship formed while raising them.
-Gabriel Garcia Marquez

Children aren't happy with nothing to ignore
and that's what parents were created for.
-Ogden Nash

Oh, to be only half as wonderful
as my child thought I was when he was small,
and only half as stupid as my teenager now thinks I am.
-Rebecca Richards

As a parent,
you try to maintain a certain amount of control
and so you have this tug-of-war...
you have to learn when to let go.
And that's not easy.
-Aretha Franklin

The only thing I ever said to my parents
when I was a teenager was,
"Hang up. I got it."
-Carol Lleifer

Party

Too late I stayed-forgive the crime!
Unheeded flew the hours.
-William Robert Spencer

Partying is such sweet sorrow.
-Robert Byrne

There are no facts, only interpretations.
-Friedrich Nietzsche

Never give a party
if you will be the most interesting person there.
-Mickey Friedman

We live in an age where
pizza gets to your home faster than the police.
-Jeff Marder

One reason I don't drink is
that I want to know when I am having a good time.
-Nancy Ashtor

Boys should abstain from all use of wine
until their eighteenth year, for it is wrong to add fire to fire.
-Plato

Have a blast while you last.
-Hollis Stacy

Passover

Let all who are hungry come in and eat,
let all who are needy come and make Passover.
-Haggadah

And thus shall ye eat it; with your loins girded,
your shoes on your feet, and your staff in your hand;
and ye shall eat it in haste: It is the Lord's Passover.
-Exodus 12:11 (KJV)

Prom
(see also Dance and Dating)

The gown is hers that wears it;
and the world is his who enjoys it.
-French proverb

Lots of people want to ride with you in the limo,
but what you want is someone who will take the bus with
you when the limo breaks down.
-Oprah Winfrey

The future is built on brains, not prom court.
-Anna Quindlen

Life itself is the most wonderful fairytale.
-Hans Christian Andersen

Life is not measured by the number of breaths we take
but by the moments that take our breath away.
-George Carlin

Rock-Climbing
(see also Excitement/Extreme Sports/Fear)

Oh, the wild joys of living! The leaping from rock to rock...
All the heart and the soul and the senses forever in joy.
-Robert Browning

A rugged stone grows smooth from hand to hand.
-George Herbert

Live each day as you would climb a mountain...
climb slowly, steadily, enjoying each passing moment;
and the view from the summit will serve
as a fitting climax for the journey.
-Harold V. Melchert

Running
(see also Sports/Games and Talent)

Even if you're on the right track,
you'll get run over if you just sit there.
-Will Rogers

One can never consent to creep
when one feels an impulse to soar.
-Helen Keller

Time wounds all heels.
-Bennett Cerf

I recognized there are hurdles
and we're going to achieve those hurdles.
-George W. Bush

Behold the turtle.
He makes progress only when he sticks his neck out.
-James Bryant Conant

A journey of a thousand miles must begin
with a single step.
-Chinese proverb

School
(also available: College and Home School)

Try not to have a good time...
this is supposed to be educational.
-Charles M. Shultz

I have never let my schooling interfere with my education.
-Mark Twain

The Write TEEN Words

Develop a passion for learning.
If you do, you will never cease to grow.
-Anthony J. D'Angelo

We all learn by experience
but some of us have to go to summer school.
-Peter De Vries

If there were no schools to
take children away from home part of the time,
the insane asylums would be filled with mothers.
-E.W. Howe

Rarely is the question asked, "Is our children learning?"
-George W. Bush

If school results were the key to power,
girls would be running the world.
-Sarah Boseley

Better to be happy than wise.
-John Heywood

Good is not good, where better is expected.
-Thomas Fuller

Seventy percent of success in life is showing up.
-Woody Allen

It is hard to convince a high-school student
that he will encounter a lot of problems more difficult
than those of algebra and geometry.
-Edgar W. Howe

I'm going to graduate on time no matter how long it takes.
-Senior. University of Pittsburgh

The person who upsets you the most is your best teacher,
because they bring you face to face with who you are.
-Lynn Andrews

The mediocre teacher tells. The good teacher explains.
The superior teacher demonstrates.
The great teacher inspires.
-William A. Ward

Life is my college.
May I graduate well, and earn some honors.
-Louisa May Alcott

Scouts

A Scout smiles and whistles under all circumstances.
-Robert Baden-Powell

Be Prepared: the meaning of the motto is
that a scout must prepare himself by previous thinking out
and practicing how to act on any accident or emergency
so that he is never taken by surprise.
-Robert Baden-Powell

Honor lies in honest toil.
-Steven Grover Cleveland

Scrapbooking
(see also Arts/Crafts, Hobby/Collection, Memories and Talent)

The beauty of the written word is that
it can be held close to the heart
and read over and over again.
-Florence Littauer

You want to make the most of every little scrap life gives you.
My mother taught me that.
-Joyce Maynard

More than paper, ribbons and string,
are memories of the heart.
-Najah T. Clemmons

To forget one's ancestors
is to be a brook with a source, a tree without a root.
-Chinese proverb

Life is not about significant details, illuminated in a flash,
fixed forever. Photographs are.
-Susan Sontag

Shopping
(see also Style)

Life is ours to be spent, not to be saved.
-D.H. Lawrence

It is frequently said that children do not know the value of money. This is only partially true. They do not know the value of your money. Their money, they know the value of.
-Judy Markey

Too many people spend money they haven't earned to buy things they don' t want, to impress people they don't like.
-Will Smith

Women usually love what they buy,
yet hate two-thirds of what is in their closets.
-Mignon McLaughlin

You can't have everything in life...where would you put it?
-Stephen Wright

A love of fashion makes the economy go round.
-Liz Tilberis

Teenagers travel in droves, packs, swarms...
To the librarian, they're a gaggle of geese.
To the cook, they're a scourge of locusts.
To department stores they're a big beautiful exaltation
of larks...all lovely and loose and jingly.
-Bernice Fitz-Gibbon

Sibling
(see also Brother, Family/Heritage, and Sister)

When we weren't scratching each other's eyes out,
we were making each other laugh
harder than anyone else could.
-Lucie Arnaz

Those who tease you love you.
-Jewish proverb

Siblings are the people we practice on,
the people who teach us
about fairness and cooperation and kindness and caring-
quite often the hard way.
-Pamela Dugdale

Sticks in a bundle are unbreakable.
-Kenyan proverb

Don't undermine your worth
by comparing yourself with others.
It is because we are different that each of us is special.
-Brian Dyson

To the outside world we all grow old.
But not to brothers and sisters...
We live outside the touch of time.
-Clara Ortega

Having one child makes you a parent;
having two or three makes you a referee.
-David Frost

Sister
(See also Family/Heritage and Sibling)

We acquire friends and we make enemies,
but our sisters come with the territory.
-Evelyn Loeb

When sisters stand shoulder to shoulder,
who stands a chance against us?
-Pam Brown

A sister is both your mirror- and your opposite.
-Elizabeth Fishel

Sisters are probably the most competitive relationship
within the family, but once the sisters are grown,
it becomes the strongest relationship.
-Margaret Mead

Sisterhood is powerful.
-Robin Morgan

A sister is a gift to the heart, a friend to the spirit,
a golden thread to the meaning of life.
-Isadora James

Sisters don't need words.
They have perfected a language of snarls and smiles
and frowns and winks – expressions of shocked surprise
and incredulity and disbelief.
Sniffs and snorts and gasps and sighs –
that can undermine any tale you're telling.
-Pam Brown

Having a sister is like having a best friend
you can't get rid of.
You know whatever you do, they'll still be there.
-Amy Li

Is solace anywhere more comforting
than in the arms of a sister?
-Alice Walker

Of two sisters one is always the watcher; one is the dancer.
-Louise Gluck

Big sisters are the crab grass in the lawn of life.
-Charles M. Shultz

More than Santa Claus,
your sister knows when you've been bad or good.
-Linda Sunshine

A sister is a little bit of childhood that can never be lost.
-Marion C. Garretty

Not many may know the depths of true sisterly love.
-Margaret Courtney

We don't have to be like one another to enjoy sisterhood.
-Barbara W. Winder

Skateboarding
(See Excitement/Extreme Sports/Fear and Skating)

Skating
(See also Excitement/Extreme Sports/Fear and Talent)

When you're skating on thin ice, you may as well tap-dance.
-Bryce Courtenay

We all live amid surfaces,
and the true art is to skate well on them.
-Ralph Waldo Emerson

A man learns to skate by staggering about
making a fool of himself; indeed,
he progresses in all things
by making a fool of himself.
-George Bernard Shaw

Our greatest glory is not in never falling,
but in rising every time we fall.
-Confucius

Skiing
(Water Skiing: see Swimming/Water Sports)

Skiing involves outdoor fun
with knocking down trees with your face.
-Dave Barry

There are really only three things to learn in skiing:
how to put on your skis, how to slide downhill,
and how to walk along the hospital corridor.
-Lord Mancroft

Our greatest glory is not in never falling,
but in rising every time we fall.
-Confucius

Sleepover

There are three kinds of friends:
best friends, guest friends, and pest friends.
-Laurence J. Peter

"Stay" is a charming word in a friend's vocabulary.
-Amos Bronson Alcott

Most glorious night! Thou were not sent for slumber!
-Lord Byron

Snow

Snowflakes are one of nature's most fragile things,
but just look at what they can do when they stick together.
-Vesta M. Kelly

Oh! the snow, the beautiful snow,
filling the sky and earth below...
dancing, flirting, skimming along.
-J.W. Watson

Snow and adolescence are the only problems
that disappear if you ignore them long enough.
-Earl Wilson

I used to be snow-white... but I drifted.
-Mae West

A lot of people like snow.
I find it to be an unnecessary freezing of water.
-Carl Reiner

The Eskimo has fifty-two names for snow
because it is important to them;
there ought to be as many for love.
-Margaret Atwood

Soccer
(see also Sports/Games and Talent)

If it moves, kick it. If it doesn't move, kick it until it does.
-Phil Woosnam

I don't like the competition part of soccer.
It's a war in short pants.
-Shakira

Soccer is simple, but it is difficult to play simple.
-Johan Cruijff

Kicking is very important...
In fact, some of the more enthusiastic players
even kick the ball occasionally.
-Alfred Hitchcock

Softball
(see also Sports/Games and Talent)

Walk softly and carry a big stick.
-Theodore Roosevelt

Don't forget to swing hard, in case you hit the ball.
-Woodie Held

A woman may not hit the ball as hard as a man
but it's different...I prize that difference.
-Louise Nevelson

Have a strong mind and a soft heart.
-Anthony J. D'Angelo

The unforgivable crime is soft hitting.
-Theodore Roosevelt

Son
(see also Boys, Family/Heritage and Teenager)

Serving as keeper of the family name and
guardian of its promise, a son breathes new life into old
plans and reminds the world of what tomorrow may bring.
-Joanne Davis

You don't raise heroes; you raise sons.
And if you treat them like sons, they'll turn out to be heroes-
even it it's just in your eyes.
-Walter Shirra Sr.

If I have a monument in this world, it is my son.
-Maya Angelou

Your son at five is your master, at ten your slave,
at fifteen your double, and after that, your friend or foe,
depending on his bringing up.
-Hasdai Ibn Shaprut

A boy becomes an adult
three years before his parents think he does,
and about two years after he thinks he does.
-Gen. Lewis B. Hershey

Who is this porcupine that lives in my house,
eats my food, and talks back to me?
I don't know, but under his quills, he's hiding my son.
-Crystal Dawn Perry

The sooner you treat your son as a man,
the sooner he will be one.
-John Dryden

Sons are the anchors of a mother's life.
-Sophocles

My son, when you were born, you brought me happiness,
as you grew, you made me laugh and brought me joy,
now you are a man, and you make me proud!
-Catherine Pulsifer

Son: acronym for Scared Of Nothing.
-Crystal Dawn Perry

It is not flesh and blood
but the heart which makes us fathers and sons.
-Johann Schiller

Special Needs
(see also Hardship)

I have never been disabled in my dreams.
-Christopher Reeve

They are able who think they are able.
-Virgil

Don't cry over things that were or things that aren't.
Enjoy what you have now to the fullest.
-Barbara Bush

I am as my creator made me,
and since He is satisfied, so am I.
-Minnie Smith

Kindness is the language
which the deaf can hear and the blind can see.
-Mark Twain

The only disability in life is a bad attitude.
-Scott Hamilton

One can never consent to creep
when one feels an impulse to soar.
-Helen Keller

Sports/Games
(See also Excitement/Extreme Sports/Fear, Talent and Specific Sports)

It should be noted that the games of children are not games,
and must be considered as their most serious actions.
-Michel de Montaigne

About the only time losing is more fun than winning
is when you're fighting temptation.
-Tom Wilson

The desire to win is born in most of us.
The will to win is a matter of training.
The manner of winning is a matter of honor.
-Margaret Thatcher

What matters is not the size of the dog in the fight,
but the size of the fight in the dog.
-Coach Bear Bryant

The game of life is not so much in holding a good hand
as playing a poor hand well.
-H.T. Leslie

The Write TEEN Words

It is in games that many men discover their paradise.
-Robert Lynd

The best lessons children learn through video games
is standing still will get them killed
quicker than anything else.
-Jinx Milea

Talent wins games,
but teamwork and intelligence win championships.
-Michael Jordan

Anything boys can do, girls can do better
and look more graceful doing it.
-Crystal Dawn Perry

First become a winner in life.
Then it's easier to become a winner on the field.
-Tom Landry

A team is where a boy can prove his courage on his own.
A gang is where a coward goes to hide.
-Mickey Mantle

Our greatest glory is not in never falling,
but in rising every time we fall.
-Confucius

Good is not good, where better is expected.
-Thomas Fuller

Don't cuss. Don't argue with the officials.
And don't lose the game.
-John Heisman

We're eyeball to eyeball and the other fellow just blinked.
-Dean Rusk

To give yourself the best possible chance of playing to
your potential, you must prepare for every eventuality.
That means practice.
-Steve Ballesteros

We didn't lose the game; we just ran out of time.
-Vince Lombardi

Spring Break
(see also Travel and Vacation)

Spring is nature's way of saying, 'Let's party!'
-Robin Williams

Spring break: a period in a student's life when he springs from his parents house and takes a break from all morality he has been taught there.
-Crystal Dawn Perry

Spring passes and one remembers ones innocence.
-Yoko Ono

St. Patrick's Day

A best friend is like a four-leaf clover,
hard to find and lucky to have.
-Irish saying

May you live to be a hundred years,
with one extra year to repent!
-Irish blessing

May good luck be with you wherever you go,
and your blessings outnumber the shamrocks that grow.
-Irish proverb

Step-Parent/Step-Sibling

When one has not had a good father, one must create one.
-Friedrich Nietzsche

We may have all come on different ships
but we're in the same boat now.
-Martin Luther King. Jr.

Taking a new step...is what people fear most.
-Fyodor Dostoevsky

We acquire friends and we make enemies
but our sisters come with the territory.
-Evelyn Loeb

There is nothing to suggest that mothering
cannot be shared by several people.
-H.R. Shaffer

Biology is the least of what makes someone a mother.
-Oprah Winfrey

Style
(see also Shopping)

Remember that always dressing in understated good taste
is the same as playing dead.
-Susan Catherine

The way I dress is the way I am...the way I live my life.
-Pamela Anderson

Know, first, who you are;
and then adorn yourself accordingly.
-Epictetus

Of all the things you wear,
your expression is the most important.
-Janet Lane

Clothes make the man...
Naked people have little or no influence on society.
-Mark Twain

The young always have the same problem –
how to rebel and conform at the same time.
They have now solved this by defying their elders
and copying one another.
-Quentin Crisp

A child develops individuality long before he develops taste.
-Erma Bombeck

On matters of style, swim with the current,
On matters of principle, stand like a rock.
-Thomas Jefferson

Fashion can be bought. Style one must possess.
-Edna Woolman Chase

Part of the good part of being a parent
is a constant sense of deja vu.
But some of what you have to "vu"
you never want to "vu" again.
-Anna Quindlen

My theory is that if you look confident
you can pull off anything–
even if you have no clue what you're doing.
-Jessica Alba

Summer

Summer afternoon-summer afternoon;
to me those have always been the two most
beautiful words in the English language.
-Henry James

If you can spend a perfectly useless afternoon in a perfectly
useless manner, you have learned how to live.
-Lin Yutang

Summer is a gift-
blue on top, green on bottom,
wrapped with warmth and tied with a sunbeam.
-Crystal Dawn Perry

We all learn by experience
but some of us have to go to summer school.
-Peter De Vries

Our friendship brings sunshine to shade,
and shade to sunshine.
-Thomas Burke

If I had my life to live over,
I would start barefoot earlier in the summer
and stay that way later in the fall.
I would go to more dances.
I would ride more merry-go-rounds.
-Nadine Stair

Ah, summer,
what power you have to make us suffer and like it.
-Russel Baker

The great duties of life are written with a sunbeam.
-John Jortin

Sunbathing
(see also Summer)

Oh, my God. I have to be so brave.
-Cindy Crawford

The beach was crowded; people tossed like ripe corn,
buttering themselves as they went.
-Anne Sexton

I never expected to see the day
when girls would get sunburned in the places they do now.
-Will Rogers

How beautiful it is to do nothing and then to rest afterward.
-Spanish proverb

Sunglasses

When I look at the future, it's so bright it burns my eyes.
-Oprah Winfrey

Our friendship brings sunshine to shade,
and shade to sunshine.
-Thomas Burke

Surfing
(see Beach and Swimming/Water Sports)

Swimming/Water Sports
(see also Beach)

Not everything is a mermaid that dives into the water.
-Russian proverb

The water is your friend...you don't have to fight with water;
just share the same spirit as the water,
and it will help you move.
- Aleksandr Popov

On matters of style, swim with the current,
On matters of principle, stand like a rock.
-Thomas Jefferson

You can't cross the sea
merely by standing and staring at the water.
-Rabindranath Tagore

Thousands have lived without love, not one without water.
-W.H. Auden

Don't rock the boat.
-French proverb

The problem with the gene pool is that there's no lifeguard.
-David Gerrold

A lake is the landscape's most beautiful
and expressive feature.
It is earth's eye looking, into which the beholder
measures the depth of his own nature.
-Henry David Thoreau

Talent
(See also Dreams/Goals/Ambition)

Use what talents you possess;
the woods would be very silent if no birds sang
except those that sang best.
-Henry Van Dyke

Life is a paradise for those who love
many things with a passion.
-Leo Buscaglia

Be brave enough to live creatively...
What you discover will be wonderful: yourself.
-Alan Alda

The Write TEEN Words

It's so hard when I have to, and so easy when I want to.
-Annie Gottlier

Excellence is not a skill. It is an attitude.
-Ralph Marston

Tell me I'm clever, tell me I'm kind, tell me I'm talented, tell me I'm cute, tell me I'm sensitive, graceful and wise, tell me I'm perfect-but tell me the truth.
-Shel Silverstein

When you're as great as I am, it's hard to be humble.
-Muhammad Ali

There was a star danced, and under that was I born.
-William Shakespeare

Whatever you are, be a good one.
-Abraham Lincoln

My lips are big but my talent is bigger.
-Fantasia Barrino

Practice your craft and make it the best it can possibly be.
-Justin Timberlake

The sweetest of all sounds is praise.
-Xenophon

I wish you so much.
But most of all, I wish you to be your own true self.
To take all the gifts that you were born with and make of them marvels of beauty and ingenuity and astonishment.
-Pam Brown

I am my own work of art.
-Madonna

Imagination is the highest kite one can fly.
-Lauren Bacall

Tattoo/Piercing
(see also Style)

I found I could say things with color and shapes
that I couldn't say any other way-
things I had no words for.
-Georgia O-Keefe

Tattoos are like stories—
they're symbolic of the important moments in your life.
-Pamela Anderson

When the designs are chosen with care,
tattoos have a power and magic all their own.
They decorate the body but they also enhance the soul.
-Michelle Delio

The censor's sword pierces
deeply into the heart of free expression.
-Earl Warren

Everyone is free to wear a tattoo or piercing
and I am free to find it ugly.
-Paul Carvel

Teenager
(see also Boys, Character/Personality Traits, Girls, Growing Up and Independence)

A teenager is…
life's aspirations, doubts, mysteries, miseries, and love,
all wrapped up and tied together with unruly hair.
-Crystal Dawn Perry

You are more than a human being;
you are a human becoming.
-Og Mandino

There is nothing more thrilling in this world,
I think, than having a child that is yours,
and yet is mysteriously a stranger.
-Agatha Christie

A normal adolescent isn't a normal adolescent
if he acts normal.
-Judith Viorst

We are the people our parents warned us about.
-Graffiti

What can I say? We're teenagers!
-Ashley Olsen

I try to believe like I believed when I was five...
when your heart tells you everything you need to know.
-Lucy Liu

Adolescence is painful for everyone,
I know, but mine was plain weird.
-Uma Thurman

Youth is a mortal wound.
-Katherine Paterson

A teenager out of sight is like a kite in the clouds;
even though you can't see it you feel the tug on the string.
-Marcelene Cox

We worry about what a child will be tomorrow,
yet we forget that he is someone today.
-Stacia Tauscher

A child's spirit is like a child,
you can never catch it by running after it;
you must stand still and, for love, it will soon itself come back.
-Arthur Miller

I wish you so much.
But most of all, I wish you to be your own true self.
To take all the gifts that you were born with and make of
them marvels of beauty and ingenuity and astonishment.
-Pam Brown

Your children are not your children.
They are the sons and daughters of life's longing for itself.
They come through you but not from you,
and though they are with you, they belong not to you.
-Kahil Gibran

I've never understood
why people consider youth a time of freedom and joy.
It's probably because they have forgotten their own.
-Margaret Atwood

Little children, headache; big children, heartache.
-Italian Proverb

Adolescence is like cactus.
-Anais Nin

Teenagers travel in droves, packs, swarms...
To the librarian, they're a gaggle of geese.
To the cook, they're a scourge of locusts.
To department stores they're a big beautiful exaltation of
larks- All lovely and loose and jingly.
-Bernice Fitz-Gibbon

Everybody has difficult years, but a lot of times,
the difficult years end up being the greatest years
of your whole entire life...if you survive them.
-Brittany Murphy

I don't like to define myself. I just am.
-Britney Spears

Mother Nature is providential.
She gives us twelve years to develop love for our children
before turning them into teenagers.
-William A. Galvin

You have a wonderful child, then when he's thirteen,
gremlins carry him away and leave in his place
a stranger who gives you not a moment's peace.
-Jill Eikenberry

Youth isn't always all it is touted to be.
-Lawana Blackwell

The difference between what we do
and what we are capable of doing would suffice to solve
most of the world's problems.
-Gandhi

Nature makes boys and girls lovely to look upon
so they can be tolerated until they acquire some sense.
-William Lyon Phelps

Children in a family are like flowers in a bouquet;
there's always one determined to face in an opposite direction
from the way the arranger desires.
-Marcelene Cox

Telephone

I know that you believe you understand what you think I
said, but I am not sure you realize
that what you heard is not what I meant.
-Berry and Homer, Inc.

Talk is cheap...unless you own a cell phone.
-Crystal Dawn Perry

They talk most who have the least to say.
-Matthew Prior

Life is far too important a thing ever to talk seriously about.
-Oscar Wilde

Remember that as a teenager, you are at the last stage in
your life when you will be happy to hear
that the phone is for you.
-Fran Lebowitz

We didn't need cell phones until we had them.
-Mary Schmich

The only thing I ever said to my parents
when I was a teenager was, "Hang up. I got it."
-Carol Lleifer

Tennis/Racquetball
(see also Sports/Games and Talent)

I'll let the racket do the talking.
-John McEnroe

Don't forget to swing hard, in case you hit the ball.
-Woodie Held

Why has slamming a ball with a racquet become
so obsessive a pleasure for so many of us?...
The opportunity it gives to release aggression physically
without being arrested for felonious assault.
-Nat Hentoff

Thanksgiving
(see also Tradition)

Most turkeys taste better the day after;
my mother's tasted better the day before.
-Rita Rudner

Something to be thankful for is that you're here to be thankful.
-Barbara Johnson

I am thankful that my problems are my own and not
anyone else's and I am thankful that everybody else's
problems are their own.
-Crystal Dawn Perry

I thank God far more for friends than for my daily bread-
for friendship is the bread of the heart.
-Mary Mitford

Happy We-Stole-Your-Land-and-Killed-Your-People Day!
-from the movie *Sweet November*

Let them give thanks to the Lord for his unfailing love and
his wonderful deeds for men,
for he satisfies the thirsty
and fills the hungry with good things.
-Psalm 107:8,9 (NIV)

Tradition

Tradition gives us a sense of solidarity and roots-
a knowing there are some things one can count on.
-Gloria Gaither

Tradition is a form of promise from parent to child.
It's a way to say, "I love you," "I'm here for you,"
and "Some things will not change."
-Lynn Ludwick

Travel
(see also Car/Driving)

It isn't how much time you spend somewhere that makes it
memorable; it's how you spend the time.
-David Brenner

It is good to have an end to journey toward;
but it is the journey that matters, in the end.
-Ursula K. Le Guin

Sometimes in your life you will go on a journey.
It will be the longest journey you have ever taken.
It is the journey to find yourself.
-Katherine Sharp

Flying is hours and hours of boredom
sprinkled with a few seconds of sheer terror.
-Gregory Boyington

Though we travel the world over to find the beautiful,
we must carry it with us or we find it not.
-Ralph Waldo Emerson

Trouble

When things go wrong, don't go with them.
-Elvis Presley

You are remembered for the rules you break.
-Douglas MacArthur

It's not that I'm stupid; I just don't think sometimes.
-Colin Farrell

Let none of us delude himself by supposing that
honesty is always the best policy. It is not.
-Dean William R. Inge

One of the great pleasures in life
is doing what people say you cannot do.
-Walter Bagehot

The strictest justice is sometimes the greatest injustice.
-Terence

When I'm good, I'm very good but when I'm bad, I'm better.
-Mae West

What's the point of doing something good
if nobody's watching?
-Nicole Kidman

There are no facts, only interpretations.
-Friedrich Nietzsche

With me, a change of trouble is as good as a vacation.
-David Lloyd George

A little rebellion is a good thing.
-Thomas Jefferson

I am better than my reputation.
-Friedrich von Schiller

What do girls do who haven't any mothers
to help them through their troubles?
-Louisa May Alcott

When you're skating on thin ice, you may as well tap-dance.
-Bryce Courtenay

Uncle
(see Family/Heritage)

Vacation
(see also Travel)

With me, a change of trouble is as good as a vacation.
-David Lloyd George

No vacation goes unpunished.
-Karl A. Hakkarainen

Valentine's Day
(see also Love)

There is nothing so sweet – not flowers,
not chocolate, not a thoughtful card as love
held in the heart on Valentine's Day
and on every day thereafter.
But the other things are nice too.
-Crystal Dawn Perry

Volleyball
(see also Sports/Games and Talent)

Ambiguity is the devil's volleyball.
-Emo Phillips

Cannon to right of them. Cannon to left of them.
Cannon in front of them... Volleyed and thundered.
-Lord Alfred Tennyson

Volunteer Work

I want the world to be different because I was here.
-Will Smith

How beautiful a day can be when kindness touches it.
-George Elliston

That's what being young is all about.
You have the courage and daring
to think that you can make a difference.
-Ruby Dee

What's the point of doing something good
if nobody's watching?
-Nicole Kidman

God does not ask your ability, or your inability.
He only asks your availability.
-Mary Kay Ash

Work
(see also Money)

More and more these days I find myself pondering on how
to reconcile my net income with my gross habits.
-John Kirk Nelson

I can't have HIS money; I can't print MY OWN money;
I have to WORK for money.
Why don't I just lay down and die?
-Homer Simpson

I was broke, but I was happy.
-Jennifer Garner

There are no menial jobs, only menial attitudes.
-William J. Bennett

In the business world,
everyone is paid in two coins: cash and experience.
Take the experience first; the cash will come later.
-Harold S. Geneen

I don't have anything against work.
I just figure why deprive somebody who really loves it?
-Dobie Gillis

Does it seem impossible that the child will grow up?
That the bashful smile will become a bold expression...
that a briefcase will replace the blue security blanket?
-Anne Beattie

If you want your children to keep their feet on the ground,
put some responsibility on their shoulders.
-Abigail Van Buren

The closest to perfection a person ever comes is
when he fills out a job application form.
-Stanley J. Randall

Nothing is really work
unless you would rather be doing something else.
-James Matthew Barrie

Wrestling
(see also Sports/Games and Talent)

Wrestling is ballet with violence.
-Jesse Ventura

Better to bend than to break.
-French saying

This ain't no garden party, brother;
this is wrestling, where only the strongest survive.
-Ric Flair

I threw him heavily to the ground on top of me.
-Mark Twain

Yard Work
(see Chores)